MW00655329

Ellie's Table

Food from memory and food from home

Ellie Bouhadana

with photography by Lucia Bell-Epstein

Hardie Grant

BOOKS

Contents

Introduction 1
Cold Plates 5
Snacking 35
Bread and Butter 53
Big Plates 75
Vegetables 129
Pasta Plates 159
Sweets 197
Fridge and Pantry 217
Index 230
Acknowledgements 234
About the Author 235

Introduction

I walked in through the back door of a well-regarded restaurant in Melbourne (which also happened to be one of my favourites). The blinds were down and it was dark, with spots of warm light cast by various lamps illuminating the room. The head chef came in, introduced herself and showed me around the kitchen. I was there for a trial and although I had some kitchen experience, I was completely out of my depth. I had not come dressed in chef whites, nor had I brought my own knives. The chef's disapproving look was obvious, and it cut me. At the same time, I was charmed by the kitchen and, in that moment, became desperate to be a part of it.

The head chef casually asked if I knew how to debone a chicken and before I could hold back the lie that was about to leave my lips, I blurted an impulsive yes. Deboning a chicken requires technique, experience and good knife skills, all of which I did not yet possess. Presented with a massive box of whole chickens I immediately regretted the lie and couldn't hold back my nerves, butterflies sweeping through my stomach. The chef demonstrated how to debone the chicken for their specific dish and I have never in my life committed something to memory with such vigour. A while later and I had prepped the chickens as set out for me. I worked through a couple of other prep jobs with the same forged confidence before I was sent home. I must have done something

right to those chickens, because a week or so later I was offered a job.

Reflecting on that moment (and others like it), I realise that I have been making it up as I go. Undue confidence mixed with an ethnic, first-generation work ethic and a magnetic attraction to the kitchen lifestyle. Learning to cook, to eat, to taste everything. I haven't had formal training as a chef; rather, my food background lies in my blended Jewish culture, my family's food heritage and what I have learnt in past restaurant kitchens and continue to learn day to day with my team in our small kitchen at Hope St Radio.

In my world, the food of the home is everything. I was raised in a mixed Jewish family, with immigrant parents and grandparents always hovering about. My father and his family are from the Sephardic world, specifically Morocco. They immigrated to Israel-Palestine in the 1960s. My mother and her family are Ashkenazi Jews, from Germany and Eastern Europe.

The members of her family who managed to survive the Holocaust fled to Israel-Palestine in its aftermath. Both families found their way to Australia at different times. Across both sides of my family there are many layers of intergenerational trauma to unpack. Exploring the food of my family, and more broadly, the food of the Jewish world, has given me deeper insights into my own history and culture.

1

Attempting to put my food into a written form is something I find very challenging, which is a tendency I have inherited from my safta Rachel. Like my safta, more often than not I keep recipes in my heart, struggling to specify quantities and instead making it the next time by feel. Maybe this is why the journey I've undertaken to make this book, with the need to record recipes with rigid measurements, has been complicated but very important for me. My safta doesn't commit any recipe to paper; she has never understood the need for exact measurements or for writing her recipes down. Her style of cooking is all intuition and the memory of women and family cooking together over time.

I think ethnic grandmothers have secrets of the kitchen that they are waiting for you to ask about. They want to talk about their past, about their recipes and experiences, to indulge you by sharing their history with you. When I ask my safta Rachel or my father's aunty, Doda Melani, about something they have cooked or a recipe that has been passed down, I always receive a story that matches the recipe. At first I get the same reaction, a shrug of the shoulders and 'oh that recipe, that one is nothing', but a couple of follow-up questions and they are transporting me to a time in their pasts. Photo albums are brought out of dusty drawers as I desperately scrawl recipes in my notepad, not wanting to miss a morsel. These stories and recipes have drawn me in and deeply influenced the way I cook and eat.

For me, cooking isn't always about the presentation of the final plate – it is the little moments along the way that create pleasure. It is fantasising about what you feel like eating, writing your shopping list, then going to the butcher and deciding on the cut of meat. It is the glass of wine that you sip as you chop the mirepoix. It is switching on all the lamps in the house in preparation for friends to show up. It is the bowl of olives you snack on while you finish cooking. It is your parents arriving at your place for dinner, eager to ask questions, wash up your mess and help with the last bits of preparation. It is the hazy delight you feel after a good meal, tipsy and rounder bellied than before you sat down at the table. Your jeans are now appropriately unbuttoned and the table is stained with sauce and wine. Those small details have always had me. They make cooking for others and yourself a pleasurable experience that is not just about the plate of food.

When I cook for others at home, my hope is that my guests feel a sense of intimacy and pleasure when they stand around the kitchen, watching and helping, and of course, when they sit down to eat the food. Having people over and cooking for them is, I think, one of the most beautiful ways to spend time with and really get to know your loved ones. This same warm intimacy and deep enjoyment is something that I hope to communicate through the dishes I serve at Hope St Radio.

Making the experience of cooking at home as relaxed as possible, both for you and for your guests, is the way to create a wonderful meal. There is, I think, too much pressure to play host when having a 'dinner party'. It isn't necessarily the perfectly roasted chicken that will leave an impression, but instead the ease at which you put your guests. You can always fit one more person around the table, you can always dig out more food from the fridge and bulk out the meal – this is something I have learnt from my partner, Rapha, and our families. Warmth and generosity are the elements that make a meal memorable, and creating the perfect spread is a fallacy. Your approach should be like this: there should be good food and delicious wines, and the meal should be well considered, but keep the menu simple and honest. The food will taste so much better if you cook what you actually want to eat and what excites you. Unlike the restaurant kitchen, there's no need for perfection when you cook at home (and I say that as a perfectionist). If the food is full of flavour, and there is romantic lighting in the kitchen and dining room, and you and your guests are giggling and saying yum, that is what cooking and serving a meal should be. This book is an attempt to put into writing my family heritage and the ever-evolving dishes I have explored at Hope St Radio and in my home kitchen. It is full of recipes, memories and thoughts that I want to share, and is an attempt to commit to memory a reflection on food moments in time. It includes recipes that I have learnt from my family, dishes that I have put on the menu at Hope St Radio or pop-ups, and recipes that I have learnt on my travels.

My travels for this project took me to Rome where I had the pleasure to cook and shoot many of the recipes and photos in this book. Nowhere is my belly and heart fuller than in a Roman market or trattoria. Together with Lucia, my friend and the photographer of this book, we meandered through markets where we argued with and were fed (mortadella panini) by local fishmongers. We spent a week in suburban Rome at Alice Kiandra-Adams' Latteria Studio cooking, shooting and eating the dishes you will find in this book. I hope these pages bring with them the scent of that Roman summer, the apricots and spicy extra-virgin olive oil.

Although in my everyday life I cook for people out of a professional restaurant kitchen, my menus are personal and reflect home cooking, whether that's a bowl of fresh pasta or a bowl of couscous with chickpeas and broth. This book is a little the same. It is a reflection of how I cook and eat with and for those that I love. Take these recipes, cook them for others, and allow your tastebuds to guide you to make each dish your own. Strengthen your tastebuds by tasting the dish throughout the cooking process. Think about salt, texture and acidity as you cook.

Nothing should be bland and I implore you to bring yourself to every dish you cook. At the end of the meal, I want you to find yourself slouching back in your chair, feeling a fullness and warmth that you can only have after a good meal shared with good people.

The belly holds a lot. It holds food, liquid, muscle, intestines, trauma, nerves. It holds the butterflies that take over our bellies when we are anxious or excited. The belly is soft, squishy, a place for a lover or child to rest their head. The belly carries the feet, and by extension, it carries us forward. Without food in my stomach I am a mess. Keep your bellies full and warm with chicken soup, marinated vegetables and oily focaccia. Cook these recipes or simply read these stories whenever you are in need of some immigrant grandma energy or a chef's snack, and fill your kitchen, yourself and your loved ones with a good amount of chaos, schmaltz and bahārāt.

FILETTI DI ACCIUGHE

Cold Plates

Matbukha with prawn oil and grilled prawns 10
Preserved eggplant 14
Marinated carrot salad 15
Blistered, marinated capsicums 17
Roman-Jewish-style fried zucchini with mint 18
Charred eggplant with tahini and green chilli 23
Kingfish crudo with a nduja and tomato dressing 24

Cute ways to start a meal

Crisp vegetables with lemon vinaigrette 29
Marinated borlotti beans 30
Grilled peaches with mozzarella and jamón 33

Doda Melani's dining table was dressed in a lace tablecloth and covered with an array of small cold plates, each filled with marinated vegetables, cooked salads, raw vegetables and peeled green chillies. Almost everything was topped with olive oil, lemon and garlic. We sat around the table passing the small plates from person to person, chatter growing as we did so. Drops of oil and red tomato fell onto the tablecloth as we placed spoonfuls of everything onto our plates. Stacks of bread were placed directly onto the table and everyone reached for a piece to swipe up every bit of flavour from our plates. I looked around and saw my dad and his cousins smiling in utter delight.

It was simple food but real food. The food of my dad's childhood and our heritage, made from recipes that have been passed down from lips long gone. That delight, and the love and excitement that we felt at the beginning of that meal as the cold plates were passed around, are the emotions I think every good meal should evoke.

For Friday night Shabbat dinners, Saturday lunches and Jewish holidays, the start of a Sephardi family meal will likely resemble the beginning of that lunch at my great aunty's. North African Jews call these cold snacks kemia. Whether at a restaurant or at home, my ideal meal is a long, slow one in which a large chunk of it is spent sharing an array of little dishes that seem to roll out of the kitchen nonstop. Each time a plate lands on the table the excitement begins all over again. Sharing these plates with friends means that you get to try everything and not get too full – something that is important for an indecisive, flavour-driven person like me. In this chapter of the book I really want to share this way of eating with you, in which small plates crowd the table chaotically yet beautifully and people pick their way through them together. Like at my great aunty's place, a lot of these dishes are served cold or at room temperature so can be prepared ahead, plated and left on the table for you to forget about until friends walk in.

Marinated vegetables, fried things and matbukha have been ever-present dishes throughout my life and now they are the foods that I like making most to start a meal. I have a number of favourites, such as the cooked Moroccan tomato salad called matbukha – which I serve with grilled prawns in a very un-kosher way (page 10). A plate of preserved eggplant (page 14), sliced, poached and then marinated, will also make an appearance on my table. Marinated capsicums are another favourite dish (page 17). Charring their flesh directly over the flame of a stovetop gives out a sweet, nostalgic scent that reminds me of my safta Rachel. Peeling off the black char is gritty work, but well worth it for the silky pieces of capsicum you end up with. The just-warmed capsicums then soak in a bath of vinegar, garlic and olive oil, sometimes with a dash of cumin too. After an hour or so the flavours are well acquainted and the dish is ready to be shared. I will also prepare zucchini in a Roman-Jewish style (page 20). The zucchini are sliced, fried and marinated in garlic, white-wine vinegar and olive oil, to which I add a handful of fresh mint.

This chapter also contains recipes that have featured at Hope St Radio, dishes that are influenced by the Mediterranean way of life. The menu is structured so that there's a bunch of small cold dishes to start the meal, just as you would begin a dinner party or a Shabbat meal with family. Diners might open with an oyster, then move on to sharing a plate of crudo before tearing open a piece of focaccia, layering it with creamy stracciatella and charred cabbage. As wine flows, romance begins over plates of vegetables and lingers over the bowls of pasta, which arrive after the cold sharing dishes. If you come to eat at either my or my family's place, we are likely to start the meal with a plate of tender carrots, cut into rounds or batons and marinated in garlic, vinegar, olive oil and green herbs (page 15). A plate of slightly smoky eggplant flesh is usually on my dining table; I prepare it in different ways, but one of my recent favourites is to char and then strip away the skin before splaying it whole on a plate over lemony tahini, topped with green chilli, the juice of a tomato, shallots and good olive oil (page 23). Grilled bread to swipe around the plate is important for that one. I also like putting out a plate of radishes, cucumbers and endive wedges, accompanied by a lemony vinaigrette (page 29), for people to snack on as the meal begins. A plate of fresh labneh (page 224) will linger close by. Borlotti beans are essential in any form – I love them so much. I like them cooked gently with aromatics until tender and served with olive oil and a bit of the cooking broth (page 30), but also spooned over grilled focaccia and topped with a fig, some pecorino and young basil. Then there are the dishes that I think are just a fun way to start a meal, like a plate of grilled peaches with jamón and mozzarella (page 33) or kingfish crudo with nduja (page 24).

As far as I am concerned, sitting at a table that is layered with an array of small plates, snacks, bites – whatever you choose to call them and whatever you choose to make – is the way every good meal should start. I hope you too choose to sit with loved ones and start at least some of your meals this way, feeling the same delight that my dad and his cousins felt when sharing the meal at Doda Melani's recently. Maybe even letting out a small pleasurable 'mmm' as you place that piece of bread dipped in the last of the smoky eggplant and green chilli, tomatoey matbukha or lemony labneh into your mouth.

Matbukha with prawn oil and grilled prawns

The word matbukha translates to 'cooked salad' in Arabic. I have always seen this 'salad' as more of an oily, spicy red dip, one that you dunk a piece of challah through to soak up the cooked tomato. I don't remember a holiday or Shabbat meal at my parents' place without this entree plate. Although a staple, it is a nostalgic dish for my dad and as such is something my mum and I make often. Serving it with prawns is not at all traditional (prawns are considered treif or 'unkosher'!), but it is a decadent, flavourful way to eat this tomato dip. If you have never had matbukha before, make the traditional recipe first (see note on page 11), then try it with the prawn oil and grilled prawns. Use the leftover prawn oil as a base for the Tagliatelle with prawns and nduja pangrattato (page 192).

SERVES 8 AS A STARTER

16 raw prawns, shells
and heads left on

2 tablespoons extra-virgin olive oil

PRAWN OIL

250 ml (8½ fl oz/1 cup)
grapeseed oil or another neutral oil,
plus 1 tablespoon extra for frying

16 or so prawn heads, left
over from the raw prawns

4 garlic cloves, smashed
with the back of a knife

1 onion, roughly chopped

To clean the prawns

Twist off the heads, leaving the shell and tail intact, and set the heads aside. Place a prawn belly-side up on a chopping board. Using a sharp knife, make an incision from the top of the prawn's belly to the bottom, slicing through the shell and meat, but not so far as to cut the prawn in half. Now press down on the prawn with the palm of your hand to open it into a butterfly shape. Use a skewer or the tip of a sharp knife to carefully pull out the black intestinal tract from the prawn's spine. Repeat with the remaining prawns, give them all a good rinse and then set them aside.

To make the prawn oil

Put 1 tablespoon of the grapeseed oil into a saucepan over a medium heat. When the oil is hot, sauté the prawn heads, garlic and onion, pressing down on the heads to extract the juices, for about 5 minutes, until the garlic is fragrant and onion has taken on some colour.

Pour 1 cup of the oil over the prawn head mixture and bring to a boil, then reduce the heat to a gentle simmer. Cook for about 20 minutes, pressing down on the heads every now and then to extract more juices. Strain, reserving the orange prawn oil and discarding the cooked heads, garlic and onion.

MATBUKHA

800 g (1 lb 12 oz) good quality tinned <u>whole peeled tomatoes</u>

1 large <u>green chilli</u>, finely sliced

2 large <u>red chillies</u>, finely sliced

60 ml (2 fl oz/¼ cup) <u>extra-virgin olive oil</u>, plus extra to serve

60 ml (2 fl oz/¼ cup) <u>prawn oil</u> (see page 10)

10 <u>garlic cloves</u>, finely sliced

1 heaped teaspoon <u>paprika</u>

1 teaspoon <u>sugar</u>

2–3 teaspoons <u>fine salt</u>, to taste

1 teaspoon freshly ground <u>black pepper</u>

1 teaspoon <u>white-wine vinegar</u>

a handful of <u>flat-leaf (Italian) parsley</u>, finely chopped, to serve

2 tablespoons <u>extra-virgin olive oil</u>, plus extra to serve

<u>grilled bread</u>, <u>challah</u> or <u>sesame focaccia</u>, to serve

To make the matbukha

Put the tinned tomatoes in a bowl and crush them with your hands. Tip them into a saucepan over a medium heat together with all of the ingredients, except the vinegar and parsley, and stir. Bring to the boil, then reduce the heat to low and simmer gently uncovered for 1 hour, stirring occasionally, until the sauce has thickened and slightly reduced.

Taste the matbukha to check that the flavour is deep and spicy. If it hasn't reached this point, simmer for another 20 minutes or so, but remember to keep stirring the sauce.

Once it is ready, turn off the heat and stir in the vinegar; this acid will help brighten the flavour of the matbukha.

Leave the matbukha to cool in the saucepan. At this point you can leave the dip in the fridge to rest overnight, if you like (it will keep refrigerated for up to a week).

To grill the prawns and serve

Heat the 2 tablespoons of extra-virgin olive oil in a cast-iron frying pan over a high heat. When the oil is very hot, put the prawns flesh side down in the pan and grill for about 3 minutes, pressing on them with a spatula. Flip the prawns and grill, shell side down, for 30 seconds, season with flaky salt, then remove them from the pan.

To serve, spoon the matbukha onto a serving plate. Lay the prawns on top of the matbukha and shower with the parsley and a glug of extra-virgin olive oil.

Serve with grilled bread, challah or sesame focaccia, using the bread to swipe into the dip.

Note: If making traditional matbukha, leave out the prawns – replace the prawn oil with another 60 ml (2 fl oz/¼ cup) extra-virgin olive oil, then follow the recipe to make and serve the matbukha, disregarding the steps to grill the prawns.

Preserved eggplant

This recipe was inspired by the marinated eggplant that Rapha and I ate at Trattoria Trecca on a trip to Rome; it reminded us of his own late safta Chasya's way with eggplant. This recipe uses an ancient Neapolitan method of short-term preservation called scapece. Just as Rapha's safta Chasya used to do when he was a kid, we boil the slices of eggplant in salted water, dry them briefly and then leave them to marinate under lots of good extra-virgin olive oil, garlic, chilli and vinegar. For a lot of the food I cook, extra-virgin olive oil plays an important role. So does a good bottle of wine vinegar. Seek out the best quality bottles you can find, especially for this recipe. It is the heart of the dish.

SERVES 5 AS A STARTER

2 eggplants (aubergines)

2 garlic cloves, thinly sliced

60 ml (2 fl oz/¼ cup) Chardonnay vinegar

1 tablespoon red-wine vinegar

1 teaspoon maple syrup or white balsamic vinegar

120 ml (4 fl oz) extra-virgin olive oil

pinch of chilli flakes

Bring a pot of water to the boil and season the water with salt, tasting it to make sure it is well seasoned.

Slice the eggplant very thinly into rounds 5 mm (¼ in) thick – this is easiest with a mandolin, but a sharp knife will do if you don't have one.

Working in batches, poach the eggplant slices in the salted water for no longer than 2 minutes, otherwise they will break apart. Take them out of the water and leave them to drain for at least 10 minutes on a wire rack or paper towel.

Meanwhile, mix the garlic, vinegars, maple syrup, oil, chilli flakes and a pinch each of flaky salt and freshly ground black pepper in a bowl.

Pour one-third of the marinade into the bottom of a rectangular glass or ceramic dish, then arrange half of the eggplant in a single layer. Pour half of the remaining marinade over the slices. Now make another layer of eggplant and pour over the last bit of marinade.

Place the dish in the fridge or in a cool spot and leave to marinate for at least 3 hours.

Serve the eggplant on a plate with the slices folded and gently overlapping, with bread and some other marinated things, cheese or something fried.

Note: You can also make this a day ahead, leaving the eggplant in the fridge to marinate overnight. The preserved eggplant will keep for about a week covered in oil in the fridge.

Marinated carrot salad

I learnt to cook this dish from my mum, and she learnt to prepare it through the many feasts eaten with my dad's side of the family. It is a specialty of the Jews of Meknes in Morocco; it's a humble dish, yet one that creates a deep impression in many people's memories. The subtly sweet, al dente bite of the carrot lends itself well to the bright tang of the marinade. Lemon juice is more traditional, but I prefer red-wine vinegar; in some parts of Morocco, caraway is used instead of cumin. On Jewish holidays or for Shabbat, this salad usually features a few times down a long table, among other small plates containing Moroccan salads. Wine, the braided challah and the Shabbat candles stand close by and the smell of the next course cooking on the stove hovers in the air.

SERVES 10 AS A STARTER

1 kg (2 lb 3 oz) carrots, peeled

1 tablespoon fine sea salt

4 garlic cloves, finely sliced

½ bunch flat-leaf (Italian) parsley, finely chopped

½ teaspoon ground cumin

2 teaspoons honey

125 ml (4 fl oz/½ cup) red-wine vinegar

¼ teaspoon flaky salt

60 ml (2 fl oz/¼ cup) extra-virgin olive oil

Put the carrots, whole, into a saucepan of water over a high heat, ensuring they are fully submerged. Sprinkle the sea salt into the water and mix. Bring the water to the boil and cook until the carrots are just tender but still with a little bite. Drain and leave to cool a little.

Meanwhile, make the marinade. In a small bowl, mix the garlic, parsley, cumin, honey, vinegar, flaky salt and a small pinch of freshly ground black pepper. Slowly pour in the olive oil and whisk. Taste to make sure the flavour is bright. If needed, add more salt and pepper to taste.

When the carrots are cool enough to handle but still a little warm, chop them lengthways into quarters to form batons. Pour the marinade over the still warm carrots and leave them to rest in the marinade for at least an hour before serving.

Note: It is important to boil the carrots whole and just until they are al dente. Don't overcook them – you don't want mushy carrots for this dish! Pouring the marinade over the carrots while they are still warm allows the flavour to penetrate more deeply. The marinated carrots will keep in the fridge for up to a week, with the flavours intensifying over that time.

Blistered, marinated capsicums

The image of capsicums charring directly over the little flame of a stove will always be nostalgic for me. My mother follows this recipe, which she learnt from her mother, my safta Rachel, and which I learnt from watching both of them. The overarching idea is to cook the capsicum, peel its skin off, and then keep the soft flesh under an acidic vinegar and olive oil combination so that it lasts longer than it otherwise would. This is not strictly preservation, but it is a quick way to marinate vegetables so they will last a whole weekend and more. It is my favourite way to eat capsicum: its skin peeled off, the flesh carrying the lingering scent of char and garlic from the marinade. It reminds me of my family and the array of vegetables we have on our Friday night dinner and Shabbat lunch tables.

SERVES 6 AS A STARTER

4 bullhorn or standard capsicums (bell peppers), a mix of red and yellow

1 garlic clove, finely sliced

2 tablespoons red-wine vinegar

1 teaspoon Chardonnay vinegar

2 tablespoons extra-virgin olive oil

Light a stovetop burner and turn it to medium–high. Put the capsicums on top of the grate so they are sitting directly over the flame and char them until they are black and blistered all over, turning them every now and then. Put the capsicums in a bowl and cover them with a plate or tight-fitting lid so that they steam and the skins loosen.

Meanwhile, mix the garlic, vinegars, oil and a pinch each of flaky salt and freshly ground black pepper in a bowl.

Once the capsicums are cool enough to handle, peel off the skins and remove the stems and seeds, and discard. I do this while the flesh is still warm, as the flavour of the marinade will seep into the capsicums more readily. Wipe off as much of the black char as possible, but don't be too precious about it, as it imparts flavour.

Lay the capsicums in a bowl or glass dish and pour over the marinade. Mix with clean hands. Cover, then leave the capsicums to marinate before serving. Serve at room temperature.

Note: If well covered with oil, the marinated capsicums will keep in the fridge for weeks.

Roman-Jewish-style fried zucchini with mint

Standing in her small garden in the neighbourhood of Monteverde, Rome, Alice and I got talking about traditional Roman-Jewish dishes. As she described the dish concia di zucchine, we crushed leaves of the wild Roman mint that was growing so well in her garden between our fingertips, releasing its fresh scent. Deep-fried, marinated zucchini is something I make in Melbourne, but I hadn't known that the dish took root in Rome's old ghettos, nor why it was important to the city's Jewish community.

In the past, Roman Jews were forced to live in the most unsanitary, disease-ridden spaces of the city, with access to a less than abundant variety of ingredients. Thanks to their resourcefulness, they created a whole new cuisine, a true peasant food like the cucina povera of rural Italy. The Roman Jews developed a tradition of deep-frying vegetables and then marinating them in vinegar, transforming them into brighter, more richly flavoured versions of themselves. Many people know that carciofi alla giudia, deep-fried artichokes, are a Roman-Jewish speciality. Concia di zucchine are another: the zucchini are likewise deep-fried, but they are then left to marinate in white-wine vinegar, olive oil, garlic and wild Roman mint. The same type of mint that was growing in the garden of Alice's Latteria kitchen Studio grew wild in the ghettos, and it was picked to toss through the zucchini. The version on the next page was inspired by my time cooking at Alice's place; it will be hard to source wild mint as beautiful as the one from her garden, but aim to find the youngest, freshest mint leaves you can. A spoonful of these zucchini, a piece of Parmigiano Reggiano or fresh ricotta, a torn fig and some good anchovies laid out on a plate is my ideal snack at any time of the day.

Roman-Jewish-style fried zucchini with mint

<u>SERVES 5 AS A STARTER</u>

1 kg (2 lb 3 oz) small to medium-sized <u>zucchini (courgettes)</u>

<u>extra-virgin olive oil</u> for frying plus 2 tablespoons extra

3 <u>garlic cloves</u>, crushed

small handful of <u>flat-leaf (Italian) parsley</u>, finely chopped

small handful of <u>mint</u>, finely chopped

60 ml (2 fl oz/¼ cup) <u>white-wine vinegar</u>

Slice the zucchini into rounds 7 mm (⅓ in) thick.

Heat 3 cm (1¼ in) of extra-virgin olive oil in a large, heavy-based frying pan over a medium heat. To check if the oil is hot enough for frying, drop a small piece of zucchini into the oil; if it sizzles and small bubbles form around the zucchini, the oil is ready.

Working in batches, fry the zucchini slices for about 3 minutes, turning once so that both sides hit the oil. Using tongs or a spider, lift the zucchini out of the oil once the slices have turned a deep golden colour and leave them to drain on a tray lined with paper towels. Continue until all the zucchini slices are fried, then season with flaky salt and freshly ground black pepper.

Next, make the marinade. Mix the garlic, parsley, mint, white-wine vinegar and the 2 tablespoons of extra-virgin olive oil in a bowl. Season with a small pinch of flaky salt and freshly ground black pepper.

Put half of the zucchini slices in a glass or ceramic dish and layer with half of the marinade. Repeat this process with the remaining zucchini slices, then leave to marinate for at least 15 minutes before serving.

Charred eggplant with tahini and green chilli

This recipe is not strictly my great aunty's, but was inspired by a dish she made for a lunch at her place. A whole eggplant, charred over the flame of a stovetop or open fire, its skin then peeled off, sits plump and round in a pool of tahini, with confident drops of green chilli salsa, finely chopped shallots and the insides of a tomato squeezed over the top. The subtly smoky flesh is the perfect accompaniment to a plate of kebabs and grilled spring onions.

SERVES 2 AS A STARTER

1 eggplant (aubergine)

½ a shallot, finely diced

1 tomato, sliced in half

extra-virgin olive oil for drizzling

a big squeeze of lemon juice to serve

flaky salt to serve

freshly ground black pepper to serve

TAHINI DIP

205 g (7 oz/¾ cup) tahini

185 ml (6 fl oz/¾ cup) water

2 tablespoons lemon juice

1 garlic clove, crushed (optional)

1 teaspoon salt

½ teaspoon freshly ground black pepper

GREEN CHILLI SALSA

1 bunch coriander

1 green chilli

½ teaspoon ground cumin

1 tablespoon lemon juice

80 ml (2½ fl oz/⅓ cup) extra-virgin olive oil

To grill the eggplant

Light a stovetop burner and turn it to medium–high. Put the eggplant on top of the grate so it is sitting directly over the flame. Leave the eggplant to roast, turning it now and then, until blackened and charred all over, about 10 minutes – although the time will vary depending on how big the eggplant is. When the eggplant is completely charred and starting to split open, take it off the flame, gently peel off the skin and its head, and place it bottom down in a sieve with a bowl under it to collect the juices. Leave it to sit like this for up to an hour – this step ensures the bitter juices weep out of the eggplant.

To make the tahini dip

Put all of the ingredients for the tahini dip in a large bowl and whisk (you can also do this in a food processor). Taste and season to your liking with more salt and lemon, then set aside.

To make the green chilli salsa

Roughly pick the coriander leaves off the stems and wash to remove any dirt. Dry the leaves, then roughly chop them and put in a bowl.

Leaving the seeds in, finely chop the green chilli into very small pieces and put it in the bowl with the chopped coriander. Add the cumin and lemon juice, and season with salt and pepper, then stir in the olive oil to create a loose salsa.

To serve

Drop a few tablespoons of the tahini dip onto a plate, spreading it out with the back of a spoon to create a thick pool. Put the eggplant on top of the tahini, and press to spread it out slightly. Drop the shallots onto the eggplant and a tablespoon of green chilli salsa next to the shallots, and then squeeze the juice of the tomato (just as if you were squeezing a lemon half) beside the green chilli before discarding the tomato flesh. Pour over a generous amount of olive oil, a big squeeze of lemon juice, and season with flaky salt and freshly ground black pepper.

Kingfish crudo with a nduja and tomato dressing

This recipe for kingfish crudo covered in a spicy nduja and tomato marinade sat proudly on the summer menu at Hope St Radio in early 2022. I love how the tomato pulp looks like little jewels sitting atop the raw fish. People were initially a bit confused by the idea of fish marinated in a salami paste dressing, but the salty spiciness of the paste combined with the acidity of the tomato and lemon just works.

SERVES 2 AS A STARTER

100 g (3½ oz) very fresh, sashimi-grade kingfish or other white-fleshed fish, skinless and cleaned

2 radishes

NDUJA AND TOMATO DRESSING

10 g (¼ oz) nduja

20 g (¾ oz) tomato pulp, from 1–2 tomatoes (see method)

1 teaspoon lemon juice

1 teaspoon flat-leaf (Italian) parsley, finely chopped

3 teaspoons extra-virgin olive oil, plus extra for frying

flaky salt to serve

To make the dressing, heat 1 tablespoon of extra-virgin olive oil in a frying pan over a low heat, then add the nduja. Fry, stirring and mashing the nduja, until it resembles the texture of fried minced meat. Turn the heat off once the nduja has crisped just slightly, its oils are seeping a little and it looks juicy, about 3 minutes altogether. Put the cooked nduja in a small bowl.

Slice the tomatoes in half, then scoop out the pulp and juices into the bowl with the nduja, discarding any floury bits of the tomato's innards and the skins of the tomato (or you can save the skins to use in vegetable stock). Put the lemon juice, parsley and a pinch of flaky salt into the bowl and stir, then slowly pour in the olive oil, stirring to combine.

To plate the crudo

Make sure the fish is very cold. Using a very sharp knife, cut the fish into 6 mm (¼ in) slices (if the fish is too soft, put it in the freezer for 10 minutes to firm up – this will make it easier to slice). Make sure you keep your knife on an angle and you cut across the grain of the fish in one smooth action. As you slice the fish, lay each piece straight onto the serving plate, allowing some pieces to overlap, but also leaving a few gaps where the dressing can pool.

Using a mandolin, cut the radishes very finely so that the slices are paper thin. Arrange the radishes over the fish, but don't cover it all. Spoon over the dressing (you may not need all of it), then season the fish and radishes with flaky salt and serve straight away.

Cute ways to start a meal

Somewhere between a snack and an entree, these dishes are cute ways to start a meal: crudités served with a tangy lemon dressing, borlotti beans marinated in good olive oil and wine vinegar, and a plate of stone fruit cosied next to cured meat and fresh cheese. Good plates to share, intimate and reminiscent of the food we serve at the restaurant, that are produce-driven and need very little work to come together.

Crisp vegetables with lemon vinaigrette

A plate of young vegetables and lemon vinaigrette creates a beautiful moment at the start of any meal. Picture wonderful radishes, crisp and with their leafy tops intact, purple-leafed endive piled high as a mountain, baby lettuce or sweet young carrots. Whatever fresh produce is calling you, make sure you treat it well. The vegetables should be washed between your fingertips before you put them, cold and fresh, on the plate. And take care to keep their original shapes as much as possible. No need to slice the vegetables into sticks and rounds – at the most, slice them in half on an angle.

SERVES 2 AS A STARTER

½ bunch (about 6) red radishes

2 small, crunchy cucumbers

1 endive, red or green, cut into wedges

1 bunch sweet young carrots

a few sprigs of flat-leaf (Italian) parsley, washed and dried

3 tablespoons of Home-made labneh (page 224) to serve

extra-virgin olive oil for drizzling

2 lemon wedges to serve

flaky salt to season

LEMON DRESSING

½ garlic clove

juice of ½ lemon

½ teaspoon dijon mustard

80 ml (2½ fl oz/⅓ cup) extra-virgin olive oil

flaky salt to season

freshly ground black pepper to season

First make the dressing. Mince the garlic using a microplane or grater and mix it with the lemon juice and dijon mustard in a small bowl. Slowly pour in the extra-virgin olive oil, whisking to emulsify and thicken the dressing. Season with a big pinch of flaky salt and a little less freshly ground black pepper. Taste and adjust seasonings if your tastebuds are so inclined.

Leave the radishes whole with a few leafy green stems intact after washing them well to remove any dirt. Put them in one section of a medium-sized plate. Slice the cucumbers into thirds, then slice each piece in half on the diagonal. Basically, you want rough pieces that have sharp edges and don't look perfect. Put the cucumbers near the radishes but with a gap between them. Put the endive leaves between the carrots and radishes, and the parsley sprigs opposite the endives. Clear a little spot at the edge of the plate, then swipe a generous amount of the labneh onto it. Pour the lemon dressing over the vegetables and labneh, drizzle with a little more olive oil and season with flaky salt. Serve with the lemon wedges.

Marinated borlotti beans

This is a simple dish of plump, marinated borlotti beans. You can build on the marinade, if you like, with whatever herbs you have in your fridge or garden; perhaps add some fresh oregano for a little warmth, or basil for a bright summery flavour. If you have a piece of firm cheese or leftover bottarga sitting in your fridge, shave some over the beans. Beans and salty cheese are delicious together, and so are beans and fish, but they are very different combinations so choose your direction – land or sea and go from there. You could also serve the beans spooned over grilled focaccia, topping each piece with half a fig, shaved pecorino, some basil and a drizzle of olive oil.

SERVES 4

200 g (7 oz) cooked borlotti beans
(to cook the beans, see page 141),
and 60 ml (2 fl oz/¼ cup)
of the cooking broth

white-wine vinegar

2 garlic cloves, smashed
with the back of a knife

good quality extra-virgin olive oil

flaky salt

herbs, such as oregano
or basil (optional)

Put the cooked beans and broth in a bowl and add the vinegar, garlic, a big glug of extra-virgin olive oil and a generous pinch of flaky salt, as well as any herbs, if using. Toss everything together and leave to marinate in the fridge for at least an hour before serving. Serve with good extra-virgin olive oil drizzled over the top and seasoned with flaky salt.

Grilled peaches with mozzarella and jamón

Apricots, plums and peaches are a source of everlasting joy for me. Piled high at the market stalls, I will stop and stare every time. When you make this dish, search for ripe peaches. Take them in your hands, sniff them for a sweet scent and make sure they are soft to the touch so you know they are ready for your eating pleasure. This isn't so much a recipe as a way to enjoy three really good ingredients together (six if you include the lemon juice, flaky salt and good extra-virgin olive oil). Buy more fruit than you need and stack the extras in a bowl – they will make the kitchen smell lovely, and you can admire them as you would a vase of flowers.

<u>SERVES 4</u>

1 tablespoon good quality <u>extra-virgin olive oil</u>, plus extra for drizzling

3 <u>yellow peaches</u>, sliced in half and pitted

1 ball fresh <u>buffalo mozzarella</u>

6 slices good quality <u>jamón</u>, preferably sliced to order at the deli (if you can't find jamón you can substitute with good quality <u>prosciutto</u>)

1 teaspoon <u>lemon juice</u>

Heat the extra-virgin olive oil in a large, heavy-based frying pan over a medium heat. (Alternatively, you can cook the peaches on a charcoal grill or barbecue.) When the oil is very hot, put the peaches cut side down in the pan and sear for 30 seconds to a minute or until the flesh is golden and has been marked by the pan. Turn each peach over and sear on the other side for 10 seconds. You can leave the peaches like this, or slice each piece in half.

Scatter the grilled peaches randomly across a nice big platter. Tear the mozzarella with your fingers and nestle the cheese between the peaches, making sure it sits snugly between the slices. Season the mozzarella and peaches with a small amount of flaky salt, drizzle the lemon juice over the peaches, then drape the jamón over and between the peaches and mozzarella. Pour over a glug of extra-virgin olive oil and serve. This plate can be prepared up to an hour in advance and served at room temperature.

Snacking

Like my safta taught me 40
Chicken livers and schmaltz onions on toast 42

<u>Salty fish and things of the sea</u>

Fried whitebait 46
Cured fresh sardines 47
Confit tuna, tomato and white onion salad 48
Crostini with stracciatella and two types of anchovy 51
Tins of preserved seafood, pickled vegetables, bread and good butter 51

Snacking is very important to me. Always has been. During busy days I like to put together little plates of salty combinations rather than eat a big plate of one filling thing. Maybe it is because of my indecisive nature and my need to taste everything. One plate might feature a hunk of parmesan, a torn piece of fig and some leftover marinated zucchini from days earlier. Another plate might have a sliced cucumber, a piece of stale baguette brought back to life in the pan then spread with lemony tahini, a glug of olive oil, and a tin of anchovies on the side. It is how I like eating and it is how I like feeding people at the restaurant and in my home. Tastes of this and that, small plates that you snack on with a glass of something.

A couple of oysters with a glass of vermouth, a bite of cheese with a glass of wine, a small plate of summer tomatoes doused in extra-virgin olive oil with a piece of focaccia and a negroni.

This way of eating can be about feeding people in small, simple ways, finding ingredients that lure you in and plating them in their natural states. These kinds of plates can become a way for you to host and, by extension, feed people without the need for planning or much thought. Invest in a big wedge of the best Parmigiano Reggiano and when you make spontaneous plans for a friend to come over, you can slice off a hunk and serve it with what is left of the marinated peppers you made the week before. Buy a couple of tins of Spanish mussels and keep them in the pantry for when someone you love decides to drop by. Remember that piece of expensive bottarga you bought the other week to shave over linguine? Don't let it go to waste: make a tub of whipped bottarga butter (page 67) and serve it with crisp radishes or, if you don't have the time, simply slice what is left of it and serve it beside good quality butter and bread. Your fridge should always be equipped with fun staples like salsa verde (page 141) and the best quality eggs you can find, mozzarella and olives, and always something pickled or marinated in a jar. These are reliable ways to snack that are also inviting and warm.

Some of my go-to snacking combinations:
→ Parmigiano Reggiano, figs, marinated zucchini
→ A tin of anchovies, focaccia, vermouth
→ A pile of broad beans and white anchovies
→ A plate of marinated vegetables and Spanish almonds
→ A plate of gorgonzola and pears
→ A plate of pecorino and honey
→ A plate of marinated capsicums and cured meat
→ A piece of baguette with tahini, olive oil and cucumbers with flaky salt on the side
→ A boiled egg with leftover green sauce and anchovy
→ Zaatar bread from the Middle Eastern bakery, lathered with labneh or tahini
→ Safta's simple jam on toast with a piece of cheese

If you need a more substantial snack, Chicken livers and schmaltz onions on toast (page 42) are the perfect option, made even more delectable with the addition of crisp pieces of chicken skin, called gribenes in Yiddish, crushed over the top. You can easily make the crisp skin yourself from offcuts of chicken skin and fat: first you render the fat to make your own schmaltz oil, and then you keep frying the leftover pieces of skin until they are crisp and golden. I love this dish, as I love a lot of foods, but my real love is small salty fish. I have been known to pull even the most average anchovy fillet from the jar and eat it when I need a quick moment of salty satisfaction. There are so many snacky ways you can serve and eat small salty fish. I can only begin to scratch the surface of their culinary possibilities here, but I want to share some ways I like to serve them as a snack with friends. Fried whitebait (page 46), dusted in flour, fried and plated with a cheek of lemon. Cured fresh sardines (page 47), kept under vinegar and oil for a few hours, then eaten with some marinated vegetables and a slice of focaccia. A tuna confit (page 48) served with very good tomatoes, layered with white onion and rich extra-virgin olive oil. Crostini spread with stracciatella and topped with two types of anchovies (page 51). A range of tinned fish and seafood served with pickled vegetables, Spanish almonds and good butter (page 51) for people to layer over fresh bread.

Like my safta taught me

My safta Rachel's kitchen is small and cluttered. The shelves are stacked tightly with spices, teapots, old candle holders, photos too. There is always something cooking on the stove and the fridge is usually too full, packed with produce that was on special at the store, as well as vegetables that she is in the middle of marinating and sneaky cuts of non-kosher salami. The kitchen is full of warmth and safta energy. I could watch my safta weave about the space all day, if she would have me, her mix of complaints, life advice and cooking tips grounding me.

My safta never had a 'fine food upbringing'. Food has always been about survival, as she didn't have much of it growing up. Despite the lack of finer things, my safta is elegant in the kitchen. She moves about knowing exactly what she is doing, and she does it with ease and love. There is also a streak of fearlessness in her. She is not preoccupied with flattery or wealth, because she has had real things to deal with – being a child born at the end of the Holocaust meant my safta had (and still has) a lot of grief and trauma to process. Her parents lost their entire families in Nazi Poland and sought refuge in Israel-Palestine. My safta grew up with very little, as her family had no financial security; they immigrated twice (the second time to Australia) and she never had the privilege of finishing school.

Cooking has come naturally to my safta throughout her life. She cooks based on intuition and lets her memory of a dish guide her. When she cooks I see so much love and care moving between her (now arthritic) hands. Her gold rings are stacked over long, slender fingers, which have spent years kneading dough and rolling ingredients together to form meatballs, pastry and more.

There is pride in my safta's eyes when she teaches me her way of making something. It is equally wonderful and frustrating that she doesn't have her recipes written down. Because she recounts most of them from memory, the details are sometimes vague and I must extract precise meaning and methods from her words, but that is the point of her food; it is not strict and method driven, it is cultural and based on taste. The fragrances that rise from the stove, the memories attached to certain dishes – each of these things have made a lasting impression on me. I feel so lucky to have grown up watching her working in her kitchen, among the scents of Chicken soup with matzah balls (pages 102 and 105), Chicken livers on toast (page 42) and jam or chocolate-filled Rugelach (page 208).

Growing up, I looked forward to coming home after school on Friday and watching my safta and my mum create Shabbat dinner feasts for our family. It is one of the things I miss most now that I work in the restaurant most Friday evenings. There was inevitably (and still is) bickering around the creation of the meal – one of them is exhausted from a long day, my safta questions my mum on why there is so much food, asks where are my sisters to set the table, and it goes on. But I love listening to it all. Standing between them in the kitchen is where I most want to be and where I feel most at ease. There is an undeniable amount of love in the room, mixed with a good amount of Jewish neurosis and chaotic energy, which has led me towards my own love of food of the home. A lot of the love I have for cooking for others has grown out of the moments I have spent with my safta and my mother in the kitchen.

Chicken livers and schmaltz onions on toast

Fried chicken livers on toast is a nourishing snack. My safta usually grinds the cooked livers and onions to transform them into a traditional kind of pâté that the Ashkenazi Jewish community call 'chopped liver', though I prefer my livers to be prepared in a more Sephardic style. My version is based on my safta's recipe, but also takes direction from my mum and how I have eaten livers in Israel-Palestine: straight off the grill, cosied up inside a warm pita. Like my safta taught me, first I fry the onions in a base of chicken schmaltz until they are dark and full of flavour, and then I add the chicken livers and fry them until they are just cooked through and still tender. Frying the livers in this way gives this dish a Sephardic feel and a richer flavour, with no chopping of the liver and strictly no mush.

SERVES 4 AS A STARTER

2 tablespoons extra-virgin olive oil

500 g (1 lb 2 oz) chicken livers, washed and trimmed of connective tissue

1 teaspoon flaky salt, plus extra to season

2 tablespoons brandy or whisky

1 teaspoon paprika

4 pieces of bread, bagel or Sesame focaccia flatbread (page 68)

tahini to serve (optional)

a squeeze of lemon juice to serve

flat-leaf (Italian) parsley sprigs to serve

SCHMALTZ AND CRISPY CHICKEN SKIN

250 g (9 oz) chicken skin (and fat too, if you can find it)

2 tablespoons extra-virgin olive oil

SCHMALTZ ONIONS

530 g (1 lb 3 oz) onions, sliced in half, then finely sliced into half moons

1 teaspoon flaky salt

To make the schmaltz and crispy chicken skin

Gently fry the chicken skin with 1 tablespoon of the extra-virgin olive oil in a heavy-based frying pan over a very low heat. Frying the chicken skin releases its fat, and as the fat slowly renders, the skin will crisp up until it is eventually crunchy. The rendered fat is called schmaltz.

Once there is quite a bit of schmaltz pooling in the pan – this should take about 20 minutes – strain the oil into a bowl and set aside. Put the chicken skin back in the frying pan with the remaining tablespoon of olive oil and fry it over a medium heat until every piece is crispy. Put the crispy skin in a bowl, season with flaky salt and set aside.

To make the schmaltz onions

Put the frying pan over a low–medium heat and pour in 120 ml (4 fl oz) of the schmaltz. Add the onions, half a teaspoon of the flaky salt and stir. When the onions have started softening and have taken on a caramel colour after about 10 minutes, season with another half a teaspoon of salt and continue to sauté. Cook the onions, stirring frequently, for about 35 minutes all up, or until they are lovely and brown and parts of the onion have begun to stick to the pan. When they are done, put the onions in a bowl and set aside.

To cook the livers and serve

Put the 2 tablespoons of olive oil and half of the chicken livers over a medium–high heat, making sure not to crowd the pan. Season with half a teaspoon of the flaky salt. Fry the livers for about 8 minutes, stirring every so often, until they are just cooked and nicely browned all over. Put the cooked livers in a bowl and set aside. Fry the remaining livers, season with the remaining half a teaspoon of salt, then set aside with the first batch.

Deglaze the pan with the brandy or whisky over a medium–high heat. Put the onions and livers back in the pan, add the paprika and stir for a few minutes so the flavours melt together and everything heats through.

Toast the bread and put each slice on its own plate. Spread the toast with tahini, if using, then layer a few pieces of liver and lots of onion over each slice, topping with a small squeeze of lemon juice and a sprinkle of crispy chicken skin. Put a couple of sprigs of parsley at the side of the plate for people to layer on the toast themselves if they want some added freshness.

Note: When purchasing the livers, ask your butcher if they have any chicken offcuts of skin and fat in the coolroom that they can sell you as well. When the chicken skin and fat is rendered it should make 135 ml (4½ fl oz) schmaltz.

Salty fish and things of the sea

My mum loves to tell the story of making me a classic salmon, cream cheese and caper bagel when I was a toddler, maybe three years old. She served it to me and watched as I began to dismantle it, pulling out the capers and salmon and placing them straight into my mouth. It was clear that I knew exactly what I wanted from the meal, going straight for the salty fish.

This section, although simple and very straightforward, felt essential to the book, as small, salty things of the sea are all I ever really want, especially during warm days. They are my go-to snack, though these days I prefer to eat them with good bread and some pickled vegetables, or dusted, fried and served with nothing more than a wedge of lemon and some peppery rocket leaves. During long prep days in the restaurant, we often make snack plates that feature jammy boiled eggs topped with a salty anchovy fillet, a spoonful of leftover zhoug, a schmear of labneh, pickled red onions and some grilled day-old focaccia. You can't really go wrong with a meal that features little fish.

Fried whitebait

This is what I want to eat on a warm evening, sun streaming into the kitchen, fingers picking at a plate of crisp little fish with a squeeze of lemon, Rapha, my parents and sisters hovering about too, ready for a salty snack. You can also make this dish with other baby fish, such as fresh anchovies or school prawns instead.

SERVES 4

plain flour

2 teaspoons salt

500 g (1 lb 2 oz) whitebait

neutral oil for frying, like vegetable oil

2 lemons, sliced into cheeks, to serve

Put the flour in a bowl and stir the salt through it. Working in batches, toss a handful of the whitebait in the flour until they are completely coated, then put them in a sieve and shake off the excess flour.

Heat the oil in a frying pan over a medium heat until the oil has reached a temperature of about 190°C (375°F), when it will be ready for frying. If you don't have a thermometer to test the oil, throw in a cube of bread – if the oil bubbles and then the bread browns in about 40 seconds, the oil is ready. Working in batches, drop the fish in, making sure not to crowd the pan, and fry until golden, about 1–2 minutes per batch.

Transfer the whitebait to a plate lined with paper towel. Sprinkle with flaky salt and squeeze over some fresh lemon. Eat them as soon as they are ready, hot from the pan, and keep frying in batches until all the whitebait are cooked.

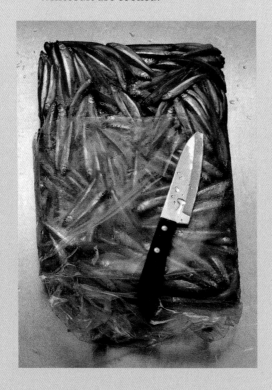

Cured fresh sardines

Curing fresh baby fish is surprisingly simple and very satisfying. They look beautiful firming up under lemon juice and oil, and the addition of garlic and fresh parsley and oregano gives the sardines a punchy herbiness that I love. When I was in Italy I learnt to make this dish with fresh baby anchovies – if you happen to come across fresh anchovies at the market, use them in place of sardines. You could also make this with other small fish like fresh baby mackerel.

SERVES 2

250 g (9 oz) very fresh sardines, cleaned and butterflied by your fishmonger (or see recipe to clean them yourself)

3 teaspoons red-wine vinegar

juice of 1 lemon

3 garlic cloves, finely sliced

small handful of flat-leaf (Italian) parsley, finely chopped

2 oregano sprigs

60 ml (2 fl oz/¼ cup) extra-virgin olive oil

If cleaning the sardines yourself, cut off the heads with a sharp knife, then slice open each belly from head to tail and clean out the guts. Rinse the inside of the belly under cold water. Pinch the spine and gently pull it free of the flesh. You are now holding a butterflied sardine.

Arrange the cleaned sardines in a shallow ceramic or glass dish, lightly season with salt and pour over the red-wine vinegar, followed by the lemon juice. Sprinkle with the garlic and fresh herbs, then pour the extra-virgin olive oil over the sardines to cover (using a little more if needed).

Cover the dish and put it in the fridge to cure for at least 6 hours, or overnight. Serve with fresh focaccia (page 60) and a selection of marinated vegetables (pages 15 and 17).

Confit tuna, tomato and white onion salad

This recipe is a re-creation of a dish I ate while in San Sebastian in Spain. In my journal I wrote of running my fork through the juices across the plate, and then, not getting enough of them that way, switching to my fingers, passing them through the last of the peppery olive oil and oniony tomato juices to collect all of the final moments of flavour. The juices were slightly spicy from the onion, but surprisingly mild, and the olive oil was magic – so deep. I couldn't even describe the preserved tuna atop the tomatoes: soft and delectably fatty, the pieces melted as soon they touched my tongue. Making your own confit tuna gives you the opportunity to create more flavour in this dish. My go-to herbs and aromatics are always fresh chilli, bay leaves and garlic to gently flavour the fish, but use whatever you love and have at home.

SERVES 6 AS A STARTER OR SIDE
DISH, OR 3 AS A MAIN COURSE

6 juicy, ripe, in-season tomatoes

½ a white salad onion

1 teaspoon red-wine vinegar

CONFIT TUNA

1 garlic bulb

½ small red chilli

about 500 g (1 lb 2 oz) sustainably
sourced fresh tuna steak

small bunch mixed green herbs,
such as oregano and thyme

strips of zest from ½ lemon

2½ teaspoons flaky salt

about 250 ml (8½ fl oz/1 cup)
extra-virgin olive oil

DRESSING

75 ml (2½ fl oz) confit
tuna oil (see opposite)

1 confit garlic clove (see opposite)

1 teaspoon red-wine vinegar

1 teaspoon sherry vinegar

To make the confit tuna

Slice the bulb of garlic in half horizontally, and slice the chilli lengthways down the middle.

Put the tuna in a saucepan big enough that the fish fits in one layer without being too tightly packed. Add the garlic, chilli, herbs, zest, salt and a few grinds of black pepper. Cover the fish in olive oil so that it is just submerged and cook over a very low heat for 15–18 minutes, until it changes colour. The oil should never come to the boil – you want to have only a few small bubbles at a time rising to the surface of the oil. It's ideal for the tuna to be undercooked at the end of the cooking time, as the fish will continue to cook in the oil as it cools. Turn the heat off and let the tuna cool uncovered for about 30 minutes. Once cool, the tuna can be kept under oil in the fridge for up to a week.

To prepare the tomatoes and onion

Bring a small saucepan of water to a fast boil. Slice an 'x' into the bottom of each tomato. Add the tomatoes to the pan and cook until the skin is starting to slip off; this can take anywhere from 30 seconds to 2 minutes, depending on the type and age of the tomatoes. Use a slotted spoon to transfer the tomatoes to a bowl of iced water. When cool enough to handle, peel the skins off and discard, then set the tomatoes aside.

Cut the onion into very thin slices and put them in a bowl for about 10 minutes covered with cold water, a few pieces of ice and the red-wine vinegar.

To make the dressing

Pour 75 ml (2½ fl oz) of the confit tuna oil into a small bowl. Grate 1 clove of the garlic that was partially cooked in the oil over the bowl, followed by the red-wine vinegar, a pinch of flaky salt and the sherry vinegar, then whisk.

To serve

Slice the tomatoes into wedges and drop them, without much thought, onto a plate. Break the tuna gently over and around the tomatoes so that it falls in rough pieces across the plate. Scatter the drained onion and pour the dressing over the top. Season generously with flaky salt and lots of freshly ground black pepper.

Crostini with stracciatella and two types of anchovy

Tins of preserved seafood, pickled vegetables, bread and good butter

Filling your mouth with the combination of a salted anchovy and a marinated white anchovy is a salty, tangy explosion you will want to keep repeating. Grill a piece of bread, or focaccia if you have any left over, spoon a creamy cheese like stracciatella (or fresh ricotta if that is easier to come by) onto it, then top with one anchovy fillet that has been packed in olive oil and a marinated white anchovy. Finish with a small glug of extra-virgin olive oil over the top. This is a nice thing to serve to a group of friends as an early evening snack with drinks – a glass of vermouth on ice to sip between bites is an ideal accompaniment.

Sitting around a table on your front porch or balcony, or rather standing around the kitchen with a bottle of good cider and a few tins of preserved seafood, is perhaps one of my favourite ways to feed people. I love that if you keep a few of these tins in the pantry, a salty snack situation can be put together very easily, in the moment. For four people as an early evening snack, choose three or four tins of good quality tinned fish from Mediterranean or specialty delis: look out for razor clams, pickled mussels, sardines, tinned mackerel or garfish. Marinated olives poured into a bowl will go well too. Setting out a selection of pickled vegetables and some Spanish almonds, along with a stick of baguette and sweet butter, turns this into an even better moment.

Bread and Butter

Focaccia 60

Whipped butters

Whipped confit garlic and tarragon butter 66
Whipped sesame seed and schmaltz butter 67
Whipped anchovy butter 67
Whipped bottarga butter with fish roe 67

Sesame focaccia flatbread 68
Braided challah 70

The days always start the same way in the restaurant kitchen: wash and dry the stainless steel bench, pull a number of long gastronorm tins off the shelf, butter them completely, then pour in a very big splash of extra-virgin olive oil. I keep the focaccia dough I made the day before in the basement fridge, alongside natural wines, a stack of sugarloaf cabbages and various cheeses and herbs. I head downstairs and come back to the kitchen with two heavy boxes of the dough in my arms. I open the lids and peer in; the dough is alive and full of bubbles. It's a fulfilling moment, to see the dough awake and ready to transform into a fluffy, baked version of itself.

I fold the dough and divide it between the buttered tins before leaving it to rest and rise in the warmest spot I can find. Then I start on making the next day's focaccia, my hands deep in mixing the flour, salt, yeast and water until it is ready to meet the extra-virgin olive oil and a long, slow rest in the fridge. A few hours later and the focaccia that has been proving by the bar is ready for me to press my fingers into it, making deep indentations, ready for a drizzle of more oil, a sprinkle of flaky salt and then a bake in a very hot oven.

This chapter of the book is centred on yeasted bread and a thick spread of good butter. More specifically, it is about bread in the form of a fluffy loaf of focaccia (page 60),

a sesame focaccia that feels a little more like a flatbread (page 68), and traditional Jewish challah (page 72), as well as butter whipped with garlic and tarragon (page 66), sesame seed and schmaltz (page 67), anchovy (page 67) and bottarga (page 67).

I like to think that the honest smell of just-baked focaccia is enough, that the taste and texture of that bread in its entirety can satisfy a person. It's simple and straightforward, but made more decadent with a swipe of confit garlic butter or a small bowl of very good extra-virgin olive oil. Of course there is a whole meal to come after, but the focaccia with whipped butter and a glass of wine might be all you really need. One of my favourite sights is seeing

the focaccia about half an hour after it has come out of the oven, sliced into plump squares. Piled on the cooling rack, they sit fluffy and tall, ready to be sent out across the pass to all of the tables for dinner. The pass is the counter between the kitchen and the dining area, where the order dockets are kept and where we place the plates of food for the waiters to collect. Along with the usual stacks of plates and oyster trays, I love sitting a mountain of just whipped butter on the pass, tall and looking almost like gelato on its silver tray. It was one of the first things I placed there when we first opened Hope St and the cooks would dig a knife directly into the mountain and swipe it over the side of a small plate before placing two pieces of focaccia beside it.

Although tried and tested, it was a tricky decision for me to include the focaccia recipe in this book. Essentially it is a simple recipe, but so much of the final result is the outcome of getting to know the touch and feel of the dough before baking it – it will be a lot wetter and oilier than you may have anticipated, but that is how it should be. Digging into the wet dough mixture, bringing the dough together with your hands, is a beautiful thing. Use your intuition and have confidence. I feel very lucky to have learnt these things from my mum, who doesn't fuss about when

cooking; she lets her tastebuds and intuition guide her. I think my mum imparted a sense of confidence in me as a cook from an early age. As a small child, I would cling to her hip as she cooked dinner, refusing to let go, enchanted by the movements of cooking well before I could participate in the ritual myself.

Just as she has always done, Mum often bakes challah on Friday nights for our family Shabbat dinners. Challah is a brioche-like, slightly sweet bread that is eaten at Shabbat meals and on festive holidays like Rosh Hashanah, Jewish New Year, when it is baked into a circular braided shape to signify a full, round year. It's delicious eaten with a thick layer of matbukha (page 11) on top and a marinated carrot salad (page 15) on the side, or you can eat it as my dad most enjoys, dipped straight into a pan of oily, tomatoey Chraime sauce (page 92). The weekly ritual of sitting around the long table with my cousins and sisters, intertwined with our parents, grandmother, uncles and aunties, feasting on challah lathered with dips and salads, is something I am forever grateful for and hope to pass on.

Focaccia

When you make a dough every day, you start to understand it: what it needs and when it needs it, how much liquid it can absorb, and how far to take it in its first and second rise (leave it too long and you risk over-proving it, and the baked bread won't be as fluffy and tall; don't leave it long enough and the bread won't reach its full potential). Making this daily at the restaurant means I have gotten to know this bread intimately. It has been tested at different temperatures, for different times, in the tin for the whole cook, and then out of the tin for the last few minutes to see if the crispy bottom you get without the tray is worth the effort of flipping. I think you can make it just as well in a home kitchen and I am excited for you to try. It is worth seeking out very good quality extra-virgin olive oil as it deeply penetrates the dough, lending flavour and texture to the bread.

MAKES 1 LOAF

11 g (¼ oz) dried yeast

15 g (½ oz) sugar

750 ml (25½ fl oz/3 cups) lukewarm water

940 g (2 lb 1 oz) plain (all-purpose) flour

43 g (1½ oz) fine sea salt

80 ml (2½ fl oz/⅓ cup) extra-virgin olive oil, plus extra for greasing and drizzling

butter for greasing

1 tablespoon flaky salt

To make the dough

The dough will double in size, so you need to use an air-tight container larger than you think, and it needs to have a matching lid. Put the yeast and sugar in the container.

Slowly pour in the lukewarm water, and as you do so whisk energetically to mix the sugar and yeast into the water. Let the mixture sit for 10 minutes to allow the yeast to activate. If the mixture doesn't start bubbling, the yeast might be out of date or the water was too hot. If this is the case, start again with a fresh packet of yeast.

When the yeast mixture is frothy, add the flour and then pour the salt over the top of the flour (be careful that the salt doesn't directly touch the yeast, otherwise it could kill the yeast). Mix everything thoroughly with your hands for a few minutes until the dough is smooth with no lumps and it feels elastic.

Next pull a section of the dough away from the edge of the container to make a small well and pour in a quarter of the extra-virgin olive oil. Repeat this step three more times at equal distances around the edge of the dough until you have used all of the oil.

Now fold the oil into the dough. I like to use the following technique: starting at 12 o'clock, fold the outer edge of the dough into the centre of the container with your hands, then do the same at 3 o'clock, then 6 o'clock and finally 9 o'clock, folding the dough into the centre each time. Repeat this folding technique twice more, then turn the dough seam side down in the container. Seal with a tight-fitting lid and put it in the fridge to rest for 18–24 hours.

To bake the dough

Butter a 30 cm × 25 cm (12 in × 10 in) stainless steel tin very well. Pour in 60 ml (2 fl oz/¼ cup) of oil – it might feel like too much, but it won't be. Tip the tin so that the oil coats the sides as well as the bottom of the tin.

Take the dough out of the fridge. Starting at 12 o'clock, fold the dough into the centre, and then do the same at 6 o'clock. Next fold the dough into the centre at 3 o'clock, and then at 9 o'clock. Repeat this once more, then take the dough out of the container and put it into the tin seam side down. Gently stretch the dough out a little but don't stretch it all the way to the edges, because as it proves the dough will expand to fill the tin. Find the warmest spot in your house and leave the dough to rise for 3–4 hours (but no longer than 4 hours), or until it has doubled in size. If your house isn't warm, turn the heating on or the dough won't rise.

Preheat the oven to 240°C (465°F).

Once risen, pour a drop of oil onto your hands and rub them together. Drizzle about 1 tablespoon of oil over the focaccia, then very gently rub the oil over the top, dimpling the surface by letting the tips of your fingers sink to the bottom of the tin. Small air bubbles should appear across the surface. Sprinkle with the flaky salt and give the focaccia one last drizzle with about 1 tablespoon of oil.

Put in the oven and bake for 30 minutes, then increase the heat to 245°C (475°F) and bake for a further 10 minutes, until the bottom is very crispy and the top is darker than gold.

Take the focaccia out of the oven and let it cool in the tin for 5 minutes, then turn it out and transfer to a cooling rack. Slice once the focaccia has cooled slightly, around 20 minutes.

Note: If the bottom is still a little soft when you turn the focaccia out of its tin, put the bread directly on the oven rack for another 5–10 minutes at 240 °C (465°F) to crisp up on the bottom, with the empty tin under it to catch the oil drippings.

Whipped butters

Butter, a kitchen staple, wrapped and concealed in paper, it is often forgotten and left to the side of the fridge. But butter is elegant and tempting. It is good on a piece of late-night toast, salty as you lick your lips thinking about the night just had. It plays an important role in creating a sheet of flaky pastry. It can bring a pasta sauce together, the fat emulsifying with the starch to create a silky sauce. There is so much beauty in good butter. By whipping room-temperature butter by hand or better, in an electric mixer, it changes form from a semi-solid emulsion to the texture of gelato. At the restaurant I serve two plump pieces of focaccia with a big swipe of whipped butter that is flavoured with confit garlic and a green herb – for a while I whipped the butter with tarragon oil, then it was leek-top oil. If you are in a more subtle mood, the confit garlic and tarragon butter might be the direction you take at home. If you feel like something more rich and savoury, the schmaltz and sesame seed butter is my way of reminiscing on Ashkenazi Jewish flavours. Try them all and serve dolloped on a plate, tall like a mountain next to fresh focaccia or a loaf of braided challah.

Whipped confit garlic and tarragon butter

<u>MAKES ABOUT 250 G (9 OZ)</u>

250 g (9 oz) good quality <u>unsalted butter</u>, diced and softened

60 ml (2 fl oz/¼ cup) <u>tarragon oil</u> (see opposite)

1–2 teaspoons <u>flaky salt</u>

1 quantity <u>confit garlic</u> (see opposite)

1 teaspoon <u>confit garlic oil</u> (see opposite)

½ teaspoon <u>white-wine vinegar</u>

<u>TARRAGON OIL</u>

2 bunches <u>tarragon</u>

60 ml (2 fl oz/¼ cup) <u>grapeseed oil</u>

<u>CONFIT GARLIC AND OIL</u>

6 <u>garlic cloves</u>

<u>extra-virgin olive oil</u> to cover

To make the tarragon oil

Bring a small saucepan of water to the boil. Pick the tarragon leaves and discard the stems. Blanch the leaves in the boiling water for 20 seconds, then take them out and shock them in iced water. Put the leaves and grapeseed oil in a food processor and blitz until smooth. Place a fine-mesh sieve lined with cheesecloth over a deep bowl or container and strain the tarragon purée. Collect the green oil that drips into the bowl and discard what is left in the sieve.

To make the confit garlic and oil

Put the garlic cloves and a pinch of salt in a small saucepan. Cover the garlic completely with olive oil and cook gently over a very low heat for about 20 minutes. Small bubbles will build up around the garlic, but be careful not to let the bubbles become too intense and violent. Once the garlic is soft and golden, turn the heat off. Remove the garlic from the saucepan and mash it with a fork into a paste.

To make the butter

Whisk the butter in an electric mixer fitted with the appropriate attachment at a medium speed until it is soft and creamy. With the motor running, slowly pour in the tarragon oil, followed by the salt, and whisk until combined. Next add the mashed confit garlic, the confit garlic oil and the vinegar, and continue to whisk until everything is incorporated. Taste the butter: it should have a sweet garlic flavour. Season further with salt if needed.

Using a spatula, spoon layer upon layer of the whipped butter onto a serving dish, aiming to create a mountainous shape. If it is too runny, put the butter in the fridge to firm up a little, then try again a few minutes later.

Whipped sesame seed and schmaltz butter

MAKES ABOUT 70 G (2½ OZ)

250 g (9 oz) unsalted butter, diced and softened

7½ tablespoons Schmaltz oil (page 42)

100 g (3½ oz) sesame seeds, toasted

2½ teaspoons flaky salt

75 g (2¾ oz) crispy chicken skin

Whisk the butter in an electric mixer fitted with the appropriate attachment at a medium speed until it is soft and creamy. With the motor running, slowly pour in the schmaltz oil into the butter, followed by the sesame seeds and salt, and whisk until combined. Next add the chicken skin, breaking it up with your fingers as you go, and continue to whisk until incorporated. Taste and season with more salt to your liking. Using a spatula, spoon layer upon layer of the whipped butter onto a serving dish, aiming to create a mountainous shape. If it is too runny, put the butter in the fridge to firm up a little, then try again a few minutes later.

Whipped anchovy butter

MAKES ABOUT 300 G (10½ OZ)

200 g (7 oz) good quality unsalted butter, diced and softened

100 g (3½ oz) anchovies, packed in olive oil (the best you can find)

1 teaspoon extra-virgin olive oil

Whisk the butter for about a minute in an electric mixer fitted with the appropriate attachment until a little fluffy. Finely chop the anchovies until they have taken on a paste-like consistency. Add them to the butter along with the olive oil and whisk again for a couple of minutes to evenly incorporate into the butter.

Keep the anchovy butter in the fridge and serve with focaccia or bread, or melt in a frying pan with garlic and chilli, and toss with spaghetti for a late-night supper dish. It's also delicious rubbed over chicken before roasting – basically, use it whenever you want to add a deep savoury flavour to whatever it is you are cooking.

Whipped bottarga butter with fish roe

MAKES ABOUT 300 G (10½ OZ)

200 g (7 oz) good quality unsalted butter, diced and softened

40 g (3½ oz) bottarga (dried mullet or tuna roe), grated

1 teaspoon extra-virgin olive oil

fish roe to serve (optional)

Whisk the butter for about a minute in an electric mixer fitted with the appropriate attachment until a little fluffy. Add the grated bottarga to the butter along with the olive oil and whisk again for a couple of minutes to evenly incorporate into the butter. If you feel like being a little extra decadent, serve the butter with a drop of fish roe over the top.

Sesame focaccia flatbread

This bread has the same foundation as the classic focaccia recipe, but without the focus on achieving a tall, fluffy rise. The loaf will be flatter than the focaccia, and taste of toasted, nutty sesame seeds. I bake mine until it is very dark and almost burnt. This flatbread looks great sliced into long pieces and placed in a pile for people to drag through matbukha or the sauce of chraime fish, or to layer with green chilli and tahini. Or you can make this flatbread–focaccia hybrid to accompany a summer kebab feast, along with a side of tomatoes covered in olive oil and zhoug.

MAKES 2 LOAVES

11 g (¼ oz) dried yeast

15 g (½ oz) sugar

750 ml (25½ fl oz/3 cups) lukewarm water

940 g (2 lb 1 oz) plain (all-purpose) flour

43 g (1½ oz) fine sea salt

80 ml (2½ fl oz/⅓ cup) extra-virgin olive oil, plus extra for greasing and drizzling

butter for greasing

200 g (7 oz) sesame seeds

To make the dough

Put the yeast and sugar in a container that can be sealed so it is airtight. The dough will double in size, so you need to use a large container.

Slowly pour in the lukewarm water, and as you do so whisk energetically to mix the sugar and yeast into the water. Let the mixture sit for 10 minutes to allow the yeast to activate. If the mixture doesn't start bubbling, the yeast might be out of date or the water was too hot. If this is the case, start again with a fresh packet of yeast.

When the yeast mixture is frothy, add the flour and salt into the container. Mix everything thoroughly with your hands until the dough is smooth with no lumps and it feels elastic.

Next pull a section of the dough away from the edge of the container to make a small well and pour in a quarter of the oil. Repeat this step three more times at equal distances around the edge of the dough until you have used all of the oil.

Now fold the oil into the dough using the following technique: starting at 12 o'clock, fold the outer edge of the dough into the centre of the container, then do the same at 3 o'clock, then 6 o'clock and finally 9 o'clock, folding the dough into the centre each time. Repeat this folding technique twice more, then turn the dough seam side down in the container. Seal with a tight-fitting lid and put it in the fridge to rest – you can leave it for up to 2 days but 18–24 hours is ideal.

To bake the dough

Grease two sheets of baking paper with butter and place them on a flat baking tray that is at least 30 cm long. Pour 20ml (¾ fl oz) olive oil onto each sheet of baking paper.

Divide the dough in half with your hands and put each half onto a tray.

Use your palms to gently stretch each piece of dough out into a long, oval-shaped loaf about 2 cm (¾ in) thick. Scatter half of the sesame seeds across the two loaves, then turn them over and do the same on the other side with the remaining seeds, making sure every inch is covered.

Leave the loaves to rest for 1 hour at room temperature.

Preheat the oven to 220°C (430°F).

Before you put the loaves in the oven, stretch each loaf out again a little with your fingers, leaving a few dimples as you go.

Put the trays in the oven for 15 minutes, then increase the temperature to 260°C (500°F) and bake for a further 15 minutes. The bread should look quite dark and the kitchen should smell of toasted sesame by now. If not, cook for a further 5–10 minutes.

Take the loaves out of the oven and leave to cool for 5 minutes, then transfer to a rack. Slice once completely cool.

Braided challah

Challah is an essential part of every Shabbat meal, and my mum often bakes two loaves for this weekly family dinner. My mum, Karen, born Keren Mandelbaum, is the child of a father who was a Jewish-German Holocaust survivor and of a Polish-Jewish mother born in the aftermath of World War II. Both my mother's maternal and paternal grandparents miraculously survived the Holocaust; they lived close by in Bentleigh and spoke mainly Yiddish and a bit of Hebrew at home.

Mum spent a lot of her childhood in her parents' sandwich shop, watching them prepare food and snacks, and serve their customers. My mum, like her mum, has always had a way with food. She has a natural ability to create warm, vibrant meals that aren't necessarily 'cheffy', but everything she cooks is made with care, intention and a lot of flavour. Cooking with my mum in recent days, I have understood that she could have been a professional chef if that option had been open to her, because of the efficient way she moves about the kitchen and the uniqueness of her flavour profiles.

The love she puts into those two braided loaves is obvious as soon as you take that first warm, yeasty bite, and the way each rope of dough loops and tightly hugs the next feels sturdy and beautiful – traits my mum and her challah share. When you make your own, remember that the braid doesn't need to look perfect – just enjoy the ritual of twirling the ropes of dough together. I love baking this fresh, sweet bread, and the few silent moments spent twisting the strands into a plait or any way that the dough feels like moving. Glazing the challah once it's baked gives it a sweetness and a gloss that will make it radiate beautifully on your dining table.

Braided challah

MAKES 1 BRAIDED LOAF

DOUGH

9 g (¼ oz) dried yeast

8 g (¼ oz) sugar

130 ml (4½ fl oz) warm water

555 g (1 lb 4 oz) plain (all-purpose) flour, plus extra for dusting

2 teaspoons salt

2 large eggs and 2 large egg yolks, at room temperature, plus 1 egg for glazing

90 g (3 oz) honey

75 ml (2½ fl oz) extra-virgin olive oil, plus extra for greasing

sesame seeds (optional)

HONEY AND BAY LEAF GLAZE (OPTIONAL)

40 g (1½ oz) unsalted butter

15 g (½ oz) honey

2 fresh bay leaves

To make the dough

Put the yeast and sugar in a small bowl and whisk in the warm water. Let the mixture stand for 10 minutes until it starts to foam up a little.

In a large bowl, mix the flour and salt together and make a well in the centre. Crack the eggs into the well and add the egg yolks, honey and extra-virgin olive oil, then whisk with a fork to make a messy slurry, pulling in a little of the flour as you go. Next pour the foamy yeast mixture into the well and mix until you have a sticky dough.

Turn the dough onto a clean bench lightly dusted with flour. Dust the dough with a little flour as well and knead by pushing the dough firmly away from you with the heels of your hands to stretch it, then folding it back on itself and rotating it a quarter turn. Repeat this kneading process for 5 minutes. If at any point you need extra strength, put one hand on top of the other as you knead, and if the dough gets a little sticky, lightly dust with more flour.

When you have a beautiful ball of smooth, elastic, tacky dough – tacky dough will cling to your hands and then release, but won't stick – put the dough in an oiled bowl. Cover with plastic wrap. If you need to, at this point you can put the dough in the fridge overnight and continue the rest of the process the next day. Otherwise, leave the dough to rise in a warm spot (about 25°C/80°F) for up to 3 hours (depending on the temperature of the room), until it has doubled in size.

Expel the gases that have built up in the dough by gently pressing down on its surface. Take the dough out of the bowl and divide it into either three or six pieces of equal size – three pieces for a simple braid, or six if you would like to create more intricate braiding. Gently roll each piece into a thick rope about 20–30 cm (9–12 in) long. Lay the ropes parallel with each other. Dust them with a bit of flour and leave them to prove covered with a damp towel for up to an hour, by which time the dough should look plump and well rested.

To braid the dough

When braiding the dough, make sure you handle it as gently and as little as possible, so the dough stays plump and risen – you don't want to overwork the gluten.

For a classic challah, plait the three parallel strands as you would your hair, tucking both ends under to finish. Carefully move the formed challah onto a baking tray lined with baking paper and cover lightly with an oiled piece of plastic wrap. Leave the dough to rise at room temperature until it has doubled in size and become plump and puffy, about 2–4 hours (depending on the weather).

To make the honey and bay leaf glaze

If making the glaze, put the butter, honey and bay leaves in a small saucepan and cook over a low heat, stirring to combine, for 5 minutes. Turn the heat off and leave the mixture to steep while the challah bakes.

To bake the challah

Preheat the oven to 200°C (390°F). Very gently (you don't want to push out any of the air!) brush the risen challah with the egg wash and sprinkle with sesame seeds, if using. Bake for 15 minutes until the loaf is deeply golden all over, then turn the oven down to 180°C (360°F) and bake for a further 15 minutes. Take the challah out of the oven, gently turn it upside down and tap it on the bottom – if it sounds hollow, it is ready.

As soon as the challah is ready, brush the honey and bay leaf glaze over the top, if using. Leave the challah to cool on the baking tray before slicing – don't be tempted to slice it while it is hot, as it needs a 10 minute rest.

Note: Challah can be braided in many different ways – there are many excellent online tutorials.

Big Plates

Seafood on ice with mayonnaise and mignonette 80
Fish cakes with green herbs and labneh 84
Whole sea bream with thyme, capers and butter 86
Chraime with charred banana pepper and green chilli salsa 90
Pan-fried chicken thighs with green olives and pearl couscous 94
Roast chicken with thyme, anchovy butter and potatoes 96

Chicken soup with matzah balls

Chicken soup 102
Matzah balls 105

Lamb cutlets with pan sauce 106
Minced lamb kebabs with zhoug, cumin oil and pickled red onion 110
Minute steak with allium sauce 114
Moroccan Rosh Hashanah lamb with prunes,
apricots and honey 116
My aunty's couscous with vegetables,
chickpeas and vegetable broth 118
Summer tomato, onion and pecorino crostata 122
On tasting and seasoning throughout the cooking process 126

This chapter is filled with unfussy, comforting mains that are inspired by moments from my life and that allow the ingredients of each dish to make a statement. The meal you make need not be elaborately prepared, taking three days to put together. I feel very indulgent just lathering a whole chicken in good butter, fresh thyme and anchovies, and roasting it until it is juicy (page 96). Some roughly sliced potatoes tumbled in to soak up the chicken fat and juices are essential, and spiking the chicken with lemon is a must. Friends will pick at the meat on the bones and at the crisp skin until they rise from the table hours later, tipsy and rounder bellied than before.

Pure enjoyment can also take the form of a platter of seafood (page 80), with accoutrements like a good home-made mayonnaise and mignonette on the side. Centring the meal around a big plate of seafood is simple in essence and definitely creates some drama. By focusing on only one or two big plates, a meal becomes a celebration of those dishes. Like a gymnast who pulls off a difficult routine, when you enter the room carrying a big plate of whole sea bream, tail and head intact, drenched in golden butter and capers (page 86), your guests will likely gasp and smile with bliss as they take their first bite.

Most mornings I walk down Glen Eira Road in Ripponlea and pass by John, the local fishmonger, tending to his stock of fresh fish in the shop window. He always has a variety of bright-eyed fish to choose from. Sometimes I will ask for cod fillets to poach for chraime, a fragrant North African dish of fish cooked in an oily tomato and chilli sauce (page 92), another day it might be a combination of flathead and trout to make minced fish cakes (page 84). I buy the fish fresh, then mince it myself with a sharp knife before adding a classic combination of green herbs and lemon. Transforming this mixture into either a fish kebab for grilling on the barbecue or a fish cake for frying in a pan on the stove is one of my go-to dishes. Depending on who is coming over and what is in the fridge or garden, we may stud the

minced fish with some extras, like chopped capers, fennel or shallots. The fish cakes in this chapter are inspired by a version I ate in Israel-Palestine, cooked by a Jewish woman of Syrian and Lebanese heritage.

When the days begin to be warmer in Melbourne and the balminess lingers into the evening, I am ready to invite friends and family over for a seafood grill. For my birthday one year (which is in April, but I was holding on to some sense of summer), Rapha and I hosted friends in our front yard and we cooked clams and mussels over an open grill in the driveway. Everyone stood around the garden, sipping beers and picking at clam meat; it was my ideal moment. I also like having people over for a driveway feast of kebabs. If you too are excited by the idea of a dreamy, slightly chaotic outdoor meal, the recipe for grilled minced kebabs with zhoug (page 110) can be the main focus of your meal. Let people hang around while you grill, and put out some pickles with labneh, crisp crudités and sesame focaccia (page 68) for everyone to snack on while you do so.

A couscous feast is a special meal to serve at your table. When they were alive, my dad's parents (my safta and saba) used to regularly make couscous by hand, as they had grown up doing in their home country of Morocco. They served this handmade grain soaked in a turmeric-spiked chicken broth full of softened vegetables and chickpeas, or with slow-cooked meat, the stew studded with dried fruits softened by the cooking process. My dad speaks of the times he would sit with his mother and watch her make couscous: the preparation of the couscous was an event in itself, one they did often. As a child he would come home from school and make a snack for himself, taking a full plate of his mother's fresh couscous and making a little well in the middle into which he'd drop a puddle of sour yoghurt. As he describes this he mimes scooping a bit of couscous onto a spoon, dipping it into the pretend yoghurt and then eating it. He shakes his head in amazement as he relives the moments of savouring his favourite childhood dish.

The way I prepare couscous in this chapter is the method my great aunty uses when she doesn't have time to make it from scratch with semolina flour. I have kept my recipe for couscous with vegetables and broth very simple (page 118), just as my great aunt (my safta's sister) made it for me at her place in Israel-Palestine recently. I wrote down her verbal recipe and cooked it as soon as I came back home, in my own kitchen in Melbourne. Another celebratory, standalone Moroccan dish my grandparents used to serve with couscous is lamb that is cooked slowly with prunes, apricots and honey (page 116). These recipes mean a lot to me. They come from another place and time, when my family had lived in Morocco for generations and cooked the food of their region, mingled with the influences of their Jewish culture. These recipes have travelled in the hearts of those Moroccan Jews who fled their country, immigrating to Israel-Palestine (like a lot of my family), a transition which often fragmented recipes as well as other cultural knowledge. These dishes are full of culture and meaning.

These big plates are some of my favourite things to cook, and have been collected from my travels, family and heritage. I can't wait for them to make a dramatic entry into your dining room.

Seafood on ice with mayonnaise and mignonette

Although very impressive and as a result potentially intimidating, a platter of seafood on ice is a surprisingly achievable thing to make. Over the last little while, my friends and collaborators at Hope St Radio, Jack and Pete and I have been finding excuses to create menus centred around plates of cold seafood perched on ice for events at the restaurant. On various occasions we have filled plates, trays and towers with everything from poached yabbies from New South Wales to grilled scallops on the half shell. We always serve accoutrements beside the seafood, like home-made mayonnaise and mignonette spiked with perfectly pink shallots. I encourage you to adapt this recipe: choose local seafood that is sustainably sourced. Spend time at the market and look for seafood that is bright and smells fresh, like ocean spray – not like the back of a fish shop.

SERVES 4

MIGNONETTE

1 shallot, finely diced

100 ml (3½ fl oz) Chardonnay vinegar

100 ml (3½ fl oz) white-wine vinegar

20 ml (¾ fl oz) white balsamic vinegar

finely ground white pepper

MAYONNAISE

1 large egg yolk, at room temperature

1 garlic clove, crushed

juice of ½ lemon plus extra to serve

1 teaspoon water

125 ml (4 fl oz/½ cup) grapeseed oil

125 ml (4 fl oz/½ cup) olive oil

To make the mignonette

Put the shallots in a bowl, cover with the vinegars and white pepper, then mix to combine. Taste and check for sweetness; if needed, add another splash of white balsamic vinegar. Pour into a small ramekin to serve and set aside.

To make the mayonnaise

Whisk the egg yolk and garlic in a bowl until pale and creamy. Add the lemon juice, water and a pinch of flaky salt, and whisk to combine. Combine the oils in a jug and begin whisking them into the egg yolk mixture 1 teaspoon at a time. When the mixture begins to emulsify into a thickened consistency, slowly pour the remaining oil into the bowl in a thin stream until you have a thick, glossy mayonnaise, whisking all the while. Season with flaky salt and extra lemon juice to taste. Spoon into a small ramekin to serve and set aside.

To prepare the seafood

First, peel and devein the prawns. Remove the shells, but leave the heads and tails intact. Run a sharp paring knife gently down the spine of the prawn – make sure you don't cut too deeply – then remove the vein and discard it. Repeat for each prawn, and then put them in the fridge until you are ready to plate up.

Remove the scallops from their shells and wipe the shells so that they are clean and dry. Season the scallop meat with flaky salt. Melt the butter and olive oil in a frying pan over a high heat. When the fat is extremely hot, place the scallops confidently into the pan, making sure they are not touching each other. Sear the scallops for 1½ minutes on each side, or until the scallops are golden on each side but still translucent in the centre. Place the cooked scallops back onto their half shells and set aside.

SEAFOOD

8–12 large cooked <u>king prawns</u>, shells and heads left on

8 good quality, <u>sashimi-grade scallops</u> on the half shell

2 teaspoons <u>unsalted butter</u>

2 teaspoons <u>extra-virgin olive oil</u>

150 g (5½ oz) <u>sashimi-grade fish fillets</u>, such as <u>tuna</u>

12 <u>oysters</u>, shucked

<u>crushed ice</u> to serve

2 <u>lemon</u> cheeks, sliced in half, to serve

Cut the fish into slices 1.5 cm (½ in) thick and put them on a small ramekin or plate that is about a quarter of the size of a serving platter.

To serve

Spoon the ice across the platter, then arrange the seafood on top of it. I like to keep each selection of seafood in their own little sections. For example, prawns bunched in one section of the plate and fresh fish in another. Lay the ramekins of mignonette and mayonnaise opposite as well as the lemon cheeks. Serve immediately, with teaspoons so that people can dress their seafood as they wish.

Note: If you can't find scallops on the shell, ask your fishmonger if they have scallop shells that you can buy separately. And if you come across any other beautiful seafood or shellfish at the fishmonger, such as langoustine or lobster, there's no need to limit yourself to the seafood I've listed above.

Fish cakes with green herbs and labneh

Fish balls, fish cakes and fish fritters are common in Jewish cuisine. I recently ate a dreamy plate of them cooked by a Jewish woman of Syrian-Lebanese heritage at her restaurant in Tel Aviv. They were served with lots of herbs and yoghurt, reminding me how much I love fritters made with fish. The recipe below uses trout and flathead, but flathead and fresh sardines also pair well. Ultimately you should choose the two types of fish that look freshest at your fishmonger, ideally one a firm and one an oily fish. I like eating these fish cakes with labneh or plain sour yoghurt, but you could also form the fish mixture into balls and poach them instead of the fillets in the Chraime sauce (page 92). Either way, serve with a bite of crisp salad and pickled chillies on the side and you will forget everything but the decadent flavours rolling around your mouth.

<u>SERVES 4</u>

250 g (9 oz) skinless <u>flathead fillets</u>

300 g (10½ oz) skinless <u>trout fillets</u>

2 tablespoons roughly chopped <u>mint</u>, plus extra to serve

35 g (1¼ oz/¾ cup) roughly chopped <u>coriander (cilantro)</u>, plus extra to serve

2 tablespoons roughly chopped <u>flat-leaf (Italian) parsley</u>, plus extra to serve

½ <u>green chilli</u>, seeds left in, finely diced

grated zest of 1 <u>lemon</u>

1 teaspoon <u>salt</u>

¼ teaspoon freshly ground <u>black pepper</u>

½ teaspoon ground <u>turmeric</u>

½ teaspoon <u>fennel seeds</u>, crushed in a mortar and pestle

½ teaspoon ground <u>cumin</u>

2 tablespoons <u>extra-virgin olive oil</u>, plus 3 tablespoons for frying

<u>labneh</u> to serve (either store bought or see page 224)

a pinch of <u>sumac</u> to serve

4 <u>lemon</u> cheeks to serve

<u>extra-virgin olive oil</u> to serve

<u>lemon juice</u> to serve

Mince the fish by hand with a sharp knife or pulse in a food processor very briefly until you have a coarse texture that is not at all smooth – you want to retain some texture in these fish cakes.

Put the minced fish in a wide bowl and add all the ingredients except the labneh, sumac and lemon cheeks.

Mix by hand until everything is incorporated and the fish takes on a slightly yellow, spiced colour. You will want to taste the mixture at this point to make sure that the fish cakes are well seasoned. Heat the 3 tablespoons of extra-virgin olive oil in a wide, deep frying pan over a medium–high heat. Roll a small portion of the fish mixture into a ball and sear it in the warmed pan. Remove the pan from the heat. Taste for salt, pepper and acidity from the lemon zest, and add more of any of these ingredients to the mixture if you think it needs it.

Form the mixture into balls about the size of a golf ball and flatten them slightly so that they take on a patty shape.

Reheat the oil in the frying pan over a medium–high heat. When the oil is hot, fry the fish cakes in batches until golden, about 2 minutes each side.

Layer the labneh onto a serving plate and top with a pinch of sumac. Place the fish cakes on top of the labneh, and drizzle with extra-virgin olive oil and a squeeze of lemon juice. Scatter with a handful more of each of the fresh herbs, then put the lemon cheeks between the fish cakes and serve while hot.

Whole sea bream with thyme, capers and butter

While I was in Rome I spent some time in the Monteverde neighbourhood. It was deep summer and I walked through the San Giovanni di Dio market, getting to know the local produce. My arms grew sore as my bag became heavier and heavier, full of plump cherries, bitter greens and delicate globes of stone fruit. I reached the fish section and was immediately overwhelmed. How would I choose when it all looked so good? Everything looked like it had been caught that morning, and there was a beautiful smell of salt and the sea. I chose a whole sea bream based on the fishmonger's recommendation, and I knew exactly how I wanted to cook it: with frothy butter to encourage a golden crust, salty capers to mimic the sea, lemon for brightness and some herbs to add freshness. Rapha, Lucia and I ate the bream prepared in this way later that evening, sipping small glasses of wine and with the setting sun warming our faces.

SERVES 4

1 kg (2 lb 3 oz) whole sea bream, cleaned and gutted by your fishmonger (or 2 smaller fish with a combined weight of 1 kg)

small bunch fresh thyme

½ lemon, sliced into thin rounds

3 tablespoons extra-virgin olive oil, plus extra for brushing

⅓ cup baby capers, rinsed and squeezed dry

30 g (1 oz) unsalted butter, chilled

1 tablespoon lemon juice

Rinse the fish well under cold running water, cleaning out any blood or veins inside the fish.

Pat the fish dry inside and out with paper towel and season it on both sides with a few generous pinches of flaky salt (about 1 teaspoon on each side). Put a few sprigs of thyme into the cavity of the fish, then leave it to sit uncovered in your fridge overnight. This dries out the skin a little, which makes for crispier skin when you cook it. If you don't have time to leave the fish overnight, move on to the next step.

Put the sliced lemons inside the cavity of the fish, along with the thyme. Brush both sides of the fish with extra-virgin olive oil and season evenly with a little more salt as well as black pepper. Bring the fish to room temperature before cooking.

Preheat the oven to 220°C (430°F).

Place a heavy-based or cast-iron frying pan or grill pan that is big enough to fit the fish over a high heat and pour in the 3 tablespoons of olive oil, or enough to cover the pan in a thin layer – be generous.

When the oil is extremely hot (be patient – you'll know it's hot enough when the oil starts to shimmer and smoke slightly), confidently place the fish inside the pan, stand back and let it crackle. Fry for about 4 minutes per side. Do not move or lift the fish before the heat has set a good initial mark on it, or you will tear the skin. When the fish is ready to be flipped, the skin should easily lift away from the pan; if it is still sticking, it is not ready and you should leave it a little longer. When the fish is ready to turn over, do so gently so you don't tear the flesh. Both sides should be golden after 8 minutes in the pan.

Put the pan straight in the oven. If you are working with fish that weighs 500 g (1 lb 2 oz) each, cook for a further 8–10 minutes; if you have one 1 kg (2 lb 3 oz) fish, cook for a further 12–15 minutes. Check if the fish is ready by making a small incision with a knife near the spine – the flesh should flake easily and be white, not translucent, and firm but still juicy and soft. You can also tear a little bit off and taste it to see if it is ready.

Take the fish out of the oven and transfer it to an oval platter to rest.

Now put the pan with all the juices back on the stove over a low heat. Add the capers and let them toast in the hot oil for 2 minutes. Add the butter and stir with a wooden spoon until it is melted and the sauce is creamy. Stir in the lemon juice and season with a few grinds of freshly ground black pepper. Season further to taste if needed, and add more juice if required. Spoon the sauce over the fish and serve.

Note: A bowl of baby potatoes, boiled and simply dressed with chopped herbs, olive oil, lemon, flaky salt and freshly ground black pepper makes a good accompaniment for the fish, or serve it with the Spring vegetables and toasted buckwheat with vinaigrette (page 146) or the Dressed soft lettuce salad (page 149).

Chraime with charred banana pepper and green chilli salsa

I grew up on the smell of toasted coriander seeds, red chillies simmering in oil, cumin-spiced minced lamb, and poached chicken and dill soup. I come from a blend of Jewish families, Sephardic on one side and Ashkenazi on the other. Stepping into my grandparents' homes was always like going back in time and being in another place. Their houses were filled with trinkets and photographs from previous lives in Morocco, Eastern Europe and Israel-Palestine.

I often try to animate these tender memories of vanished worlds in my cooking. I have spent time asking my aunties and family about the food of their Moroccan home. I pore over old recipes with my grandmother, who now lives a few streets away in Melbourne. Jewish food is vast and wonderful; it has many homes, including the one I grew up in.

This recipe for chraime feels like an heirloom. A staple in many North African Jewish homes, this fragrant dish of fish cooked in an oily tomato and chilli sauce is one that I have eaten with my family at Friday night Shabbat dinners and on Jewish holidays throughout my life. During one of the 2021 lockdowns when restaurant service was limited to outside dining, I made fish balls in chraime sauce and served them in fresh pita that my friend Pete had made. It was a weird and wonderful moment, feeding people a dish I had only ever eaten in my home or the homes of my Sephardic friends. Traditionally the fish is poached in the red sauce, but I love getting a really crispy skin on the fillet by searing it hard in a very hot frying pan, then placing it skin side up in the sauce to finish cooking.

Chraime with charred banana pepper and green chilli salsa

SERVES 6

CHRAIME

6 cod fillets, skin on (you can also use skin-on flathead or another firm white fish)

125 ml (4 fl oz/½ cup) extra-virgin olive oil, plus extra for frying

8 garlic cloves, very finely sliced

1 green chilli, finely chopped

1 red chilli, finely chopped

½ bunch coriander (cilantro) stems finely chopped (reserve the leaves for the salsa)

1 tablespoon ground cumin

2 teaspoons bahārāt

1 tablespoon smoked paprika

1 teaspoon ground turmeric

2 tablespoons sweet paprika

½ teaspoon ground coriander

1 teaspoon salt

¼ teaspoon freshly ground black pepper

125 g (4½ oz/½ cup) double concentrated tomato paste

500 ml (17 fl oz/2 cups) water

pinch of chilli flakes (optional)

To make the chraime

Wash the fish and pat it completely dry with paper towel. Season both sides of the fish with flaky salt and leave to rest in the fridge uncovered, overnight if you can. Bring the fish to room temperature by taking it out of the fridge 30 minutes before you want to cook it.

Heat the extra-virgin olive oil in a wide frying pan over a low heat, then gently sauté the garlic, green and red chillies, and the coriander stems for about a minute. When the garlic has turned a golden colour and smells fragrant, add the dried spices along with the teaspoon of salt and quarter teaspoon of pepper. Mix everything together and fry until the spices smell beautifully fragrant and toasty.

Add the tomato paste to the pan and stir. Cook for 5–10 minutes or until the tomato paste has taken on a deep red colour and thickened to form an oily paste. Add more olive oil a drop at a time if the paste looks too dry (I usually add another 2 tablespoons at this point) and stir. Slowly pour in the water to loosen the paste until you arrive at a consistency that is somewhere between a paste and an oily, loose sauce (you may not need to use all the water).

Increase the heat to medium and bring the sauce to a fast simmer for 2 minutes, then return the heat to low and keep the sauce at a low steady simmer until the taste of the tomato paste has mellowed and the sauce tastes deep and spicy – this should take about 10 minutes. Add more water if the sauce is reducing too much or starting to burn. Taste and season with salt and freshly ground black pepper, and the pinch of chilli flakes for extra heat, if you like. Keep the sauce covered and either off or at a low simmer until the fish is ready.

Place a heavy-based or cast-iron frying pan over a medium–high heat and pour in enough olive oil to cover the pan (about 2 tablespoons). When the oil is searing hot (be patient – you'll know it's hot enough when the oil starts to shimmer and smoke slightly), confidently place the first couple of fish fillets skin side down in the pan, standing back while they crackle. Fry the fish in batches, adding new oil to the pan for each batch and seasoning the flesh lightly with flaky salt. Fry each fillet until you can easily lift the skin off the pan with a spatula, about 4–5 minutes. Do not move or lift the fish before the heat has set a good initial mark on it, or you will tear the skin. Flip the fish carefully and fry on the other side until it is just cooked through, about 2–3 more minutes. Season the skin lightly with flaky salt.

CHARRED BANANA PEPPER AND GREEN CHILLI SALSA

1 tablespoon extra-virgin olive oil, plus 80 ml (2½ fl oz/⅓ cup)

3 banana peppers

1 green chilli, seeds left in, finely diced

½ bunch coriander (cilantro), leaves picked and finely chopped (reserve the stems for the chraime)

¼ bunch flat-leaf (Italian) parsley, leaves picked and finely chopped

juice of ½ lemon

Bring the spiced tomato sauce back to a gentle simmer over a low heat (if the sauce looks too thick add another 125 ml/4 fl oz/½ cup of water and stir). Put the cooked fish skin side up in the sauce – try to keep the skin of the fish untouched by the sauce to keep it crispy. Turn the heat off and let the fish rest and cook through in the pan for 5 minutes.

To make the charred banana pepper and green chilli salsa

Put a heavy-based or cast-iron frying pan over a high heat. Pour 1 tablespoon of the olive oil into the pan and when it is searing hot, add the banana peppers. Turn the peppers every now and then, taking care not to burn yourself as they may spit and pop. Fry for 2–4 minutes, until they are well charred on all sides but still have a good amount of their natural lime yellow colour remaining. Remove from heat and once the banana peppers have cooled a little, finely chop them to create a texture that when mixed with oil will resemble salsa.

Mix the chopped peppers, green chilli, fresh coriander, parsley and lemon juice in a bowl. Pour in enough of the olive oil to create the consistency of a salsa (you might not need all 80 ml/2½ fl oz), season with salt and pepper and stir so that the ingredients are well mixed. Leave the sauce to rest for at least 30 minutes so the flavours intensify.

To serve

Serve the chraime while hot, with the salsa on the side and a piece of Braided challah (page 72) or Sesame focaccia flatbread (page 68) to mop up the sauce with.

Pan-fried chicken thighs
with green olives and pearl couscous

A while ago I was on the couch reading one of my favourites, Claudia Roden, and as often happens when reading her words, she made me want to cook. My craving at that moment was for some combination of green olives and simple, fragrant chicken, the olives nestled between the pieces of meat. The pairing of chicken and olives is a classic combination. In this recipe, the pearl couscous soaks up the savoury juices that fill the bottom of the pan. I buy some very good chicken thighs on the bone from my local butcher and brown them until a thick crust forms on the skin. A big splash of dry white combined with pungent garlic and green chilli creates an undeniably flavour-filled scent that fills the kitchen and encourages the pouring of my own glass of wine. I serve this dish with marinated peppers and something green.

SERVES 6

6 bone-in chicken thighs, skin on

2 tablespoons extra-virgin olive oil

4 jalapeño chillies

200 g (7 oz) Sicilian olives

125 ml (4 fl oz/½ cup) white wine

juice of ½ lemon

500 ml (17 fl oz/2 cups) Chicken stock (page 228)

170 g (6 oz/1 cup) pearl couscous

handful of flat-leaf (Italian) parsley, roughly chopped, to serve

SAUCE

6 garlic cloves, finely sliced

3 anchovies packed in olive oil, roughly chopped

handful of flat-leaf (Italian) parsley, leaves picked and roughly chopped

1 teaspoon ground turmeric

2 teaspoons honey

juice of 1 lemon

125 ml (4 fl oz/½ cup) extra-virgin olive oil

Preheat the oven to 200°C (390°F).

Season the chicken thighs with salt and pepper, then leave them to rest in the fridge, uncovered, for at least 4 hours or overnight.

To make the sauce, combine all of the ingredients in a small bowl, together with a generous pinch of flaky salt and freshly ground black pepper.

Next, cook the chicken. Heat the extra-virgin olive oil in a cast-iron or heavy-based frying pan over a medium–high heat until it is searing hot. Brown the chicken thighs skin side down until the skin is golden and crisp, about 10 minutes, then turn them over and brown the other side for a further 5 minutes. Be careful not to overcrowd the pan. Remove the chicken and set aside.

Reduce the heat to medium and sauté the jalapeños and olives for about 2 minutes.

Deglaze the pan with the white wine and lemon juice, scraping any bits stuck to the bottom of the pan into the liquid. Simmer for about a minute to cook off the alcohol.

Pour in the chicken stock and the pearl couscous. Return the chicken thighs to the pan, nestling them among the grains of couscous, and pour the sauce over the whole thing. Bring to a gentle simmer for 2 minutes, then put the uncovered pan into the oven for 30 minutes until the chicken is cooked through and the stock has been absorbed by the couscous.

Serve the chicken pieces and couscous while piping hot on individual plates, drizzled with spoonfuls of the sauce that remains in the pan. Shower each serving with the parsley.

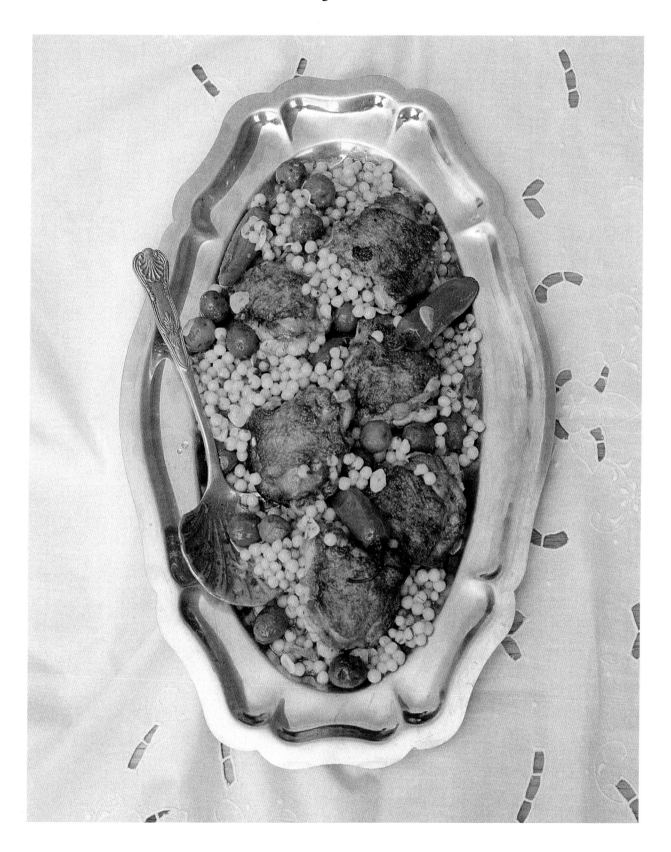

Roast chicken with thyme, anchovy butter and potatoes

A good roast chicken recipe is important to have in one's repertoire. I think about roast chicken a lot, and I am always interested in hearing how people cook theirs – there are so many ways to go about it. It seems a simple thing to make, and some people may even silently question your choice to serve it at a dinner party at all, but don't let that deter you. When it is done well, people will understand. Lathering anchovy butter over the entirety of the chicken is a secret chef's seasoning that no one expects. The anchovies melt into the chicken, leaving it with a deep savouriness that penetrates the meat. The skin becomes golden brown and crisp, the flesh tender and juicy all the way through, and everyone's lips will be wet from the complete deliciousness of it all.

SERVES 4–5

3 thyme sprigs

50 g (1¾ oz) fine salt

1.5 kg (3 lb 5 oz) whole chicken

½ lemon

6 garlic cloves, peeled and smashed with the back of a knife

extra-virgin olive oil for drizzling

POTATOES

4 desiree potatoes

60 ml (2 fl oz/¼ cup) extra-virgin olive oil

6 garlic cloves, peeled and smashed with the back of a knife

ANCHOVY BUTTER

8 (30 g/1 oz) anchovies, packed in olive oil

60 g (2 oz) unsalted butter, softened

To prepare the chicken

Pick the leaves off two of the thyme sprigs, and mix them with the salt in a small bowl.

Put the chicken on a plate or in a shallow container and sprinkle with the thyme salt, patting it over the whole chicken, front and back. Leave the salted chicken uncovered in the fridge for at least 4 hours or ideally overnight.

To make the potatoes

Put the potatoes in a saucepan of salted water over a medium–high heat. Bring the water to the boil and cook until the potatoes are only just cooked through, about 20 minutes – when you insert a skewer into the flesh it should still feel slightly firm.

Drain the potatoes and cut them into rough 1.5 cm (½ in) chunks, then put them back in the saucepan and shake it around to roughen them up. This helps to give texture to the potato flesh, creating golden, crispy potatoes. Pour over the extra-virgin olive oil, add the smashed garlic cloves, season with a pinch of flaky salt and toss together. Set aside or put them in the fridge, until you are ready to put the chicken in the oven.

To make the anchovy butter

Roughly chop the anchovies until they are almost a paste. With a wooden spoon, mix the anchovies and the softened butter in a bowl until the anchovies are well incorporated.

To cook the chicken and serve

Take the chicken out of the fridge 30 minutes to 1 hour before you are ready to put it in the oven.

Preheat the oven to 245°C (475°F).

The chicken will have released a lot of liquid overnight, so pat the chicken completely dry using paper towels, wiping the leftover salt off the chicken as you do so. Rub the anchovy butter all over the chicken and as much as possible under the skin without tearing it. Put the chicken in a medium sized roasting tin and squeeze over the juice from the lemon half, then place it into the cavity along with the smashed garlic cloves and remaining sprig of thyme. Drizzle the chicken lightly with olive oil.

Put the chicken into the oven for 15 minutes, then take it out and baste it with the juices that have run into the tin. Add the potatoes and, when you return the tin to the oven, turn it around so that the chicken is sitting in the opposite direction to before. Turn the oven down to 220°C (430°F) and cook for a further 35–45 minutes.

Take the chicken out of the oven and carve or cut the chicken or pull it apart in the roasting tin, letting the pieces mix with the buttery pan juices and tender, crispy potatoes.

Note: Desiree potatoes are a good choice for roasting and boiling because of their medium starch content, which means they won't fall apart when you cook them using these methods. Any other all-purpose potato variety will work too.

Chicken soup with matzah balls

This soup is perhaps one of the most nostalgic dishes for Jewish people, a foundation of Friday night and high holiday meals.

Although in the Sephardic world chicken soup does not have as much cultural significance as it does in Ashkenazi culture, Claudia Roden has written about North African versions served with couscous or semolina dumplings, and the addition of saffron or turmeric for colour.

As a child, I would stand by my grandmother, safta Rachel, and my mother while they prepared food for the Jewish holidays. I would breathe in the smell of simmering chicken soup and watch on as together they buried their fingers into a mountain of matzah ball mixture, rolling the balls between their palms to fill the pot of simmering soup. There was something iconic about the way they moved about the kitchen creating these high holiday meals.

Although my recipe for chicken soup is a little different to my grandmother's, it is based on her recipe. A few sprigs of dill, some yellow leaves from the heart of the celery and a pinch of black pepper over the top of each bowl add brightness in my version, and the poached carrot is essential. Matzah balls, or kneidlach, are a traditional addition during certain high holidays, such as Passover and Rosh Hashanah. Many Jewish families eat the soup with lokshen (dried Jewish angel hair pasta) and mandlen (pastry croutons); you can find these ingredients at kosher delis.

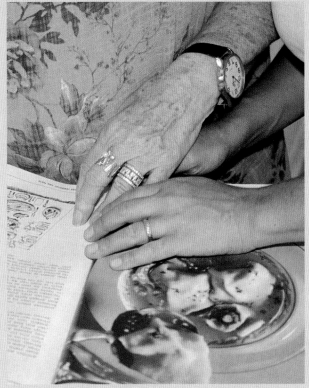

Chicken soup

I am not sure that there is anything cosier or more beautiful than a big pot of chicken soup simmering on the stove. The broth sits on the stove all day, gently warming your home with the scent of carrot, celery, onion and dill. Chicken necks are essential to this rich broth.

MAKES ABOUT 4 LITRES/
SERVES ABOUT 8

3 kg (6 lb 10 oz) mix of <u>raw
chicken carcasses</u>, including
<u>chicken necks</u> and <u>marrow bones</u>

100 g (3½ oz) <u>butter</u> (optional;
to keep this recipe kosher,
substitute 170 ml/5½ fl oz/
⅔ cup <u>extra-virgin olive oil</u>)

30 ml (1 fl oz) <u>extra-virgin olive oil</u>

3 <u>onions</u>, finely diced (set
aside the onion skins)

½ bunch <u>celery</u>, finely diced
(reserve the inner leaves of the
celery heart for garnish)

3 <u>carrots</u>, peeled and finely diced

2 tablespoons <u>peppercorns</u>

6 <u>bay leaves</u>

1 <u>garlic bulb</u>, sliced in
half horizontally

5 litres (169 fl oz/20 cups) <u>cold water</u>

½ bunch <u>flat-leaf (Italian) parsley</u>

1 bunch <u>dill</u> (set aside a
few sprigs for garnish)

3 extra <u>carrots</u>, peeled, sliced
on an angle into 3–4 pieces

<u>extra-virgin olive oil</u> to serve

Note: The onion skins give the
broth a golden hue.

First clean the chicken carcasses just like my grandmother taught me. Cover the chicken in a generous amount of salt and let stand for 10 minutes. Rinse off the salt and place the chicken in a bowl. Cover with tap water and leave for another 10 minutes, then drain and set aside.

Over a medium heat, melt the butter and warm the extra-virgin olive oil in a large stockpot – it needs to be big enough to hold all the ingredients listed, plus 5 litres of water. Put the onions, celery and finely diced carrots in the pot, together with the peppercorns and bay leaves, and sweat the vegetables for around 15 minutes.

Once the vegetables have softened and smell fragrant, add the garlic and stir. Season with a small amount of salt.

Put the chicken carcasses in the pot (be mindful about contamination – soap down any surface that comes into contact with the raw chicken) and the onion skins, then cover with the cold water.

Bring to the boil, then reduce to a gentle simmer. Cook for at least 3 hours (between 3 and 5 hours is ideal). Refrain from stirring the soup during that time: the less you stir, the clearer the final broth will be. Skim off any foam that forms on the surface.

After about 2 hours of cooking the soup, season further with salt and put the bunches of parsley and dill in the pot. Gently push them down so they sit just under the surface. Add the extra carrots to the soup at this point and poach them for about 10 minutes, until they are tender. Lift them out and set them aside until you are ready to serve.

When the broth is golden, full of flavour and not watery, strain it and discard the solids. Season the broth further to taste if needed, cool and refrigerate. Once it cools there will be a layer of hard yellow fat on the top of the soup. Lift this fat cap off before serving (you can save it to rub over chicken, to cook potatoes in or to add to ragus for extra flavour).

To serve, fill each bowl with two ladles of soup and a piece of poached carrot. Top with the dill and celery leaves, a small pinch of flaky salt and freshly ground black pepper, and a few drops of olive oil.

Matzah balls

Although you can eat a bowl of chicken soup on its own, or with kosher noodles or angel hair pasta, I think you should spend a little extra time making schmaltzy, grieben-studded matzah balls because they are delicious and iconic. A kind of fluffy Jewish dumpling, the balls are served in the chicken soup, where they will look like they are dancing in the golden liquid – a satisfying process.

MAKES 30–40

2 onions, finely chopped

1 tablespoon extra-virgin olive oil, plus extra splashes

375 g (13 oz) coarse matzah meal

810 ml (27½ fl oz/3¼ cups) warm water

½ tablespoon stock powder, undissolved

5 eggs

75 ml (2½ fl oz) schmaltz (either store bought or make your own – see page 42; or substitute with 3 tablespoons extra-virgin olive oil)

On a low–medium heat, fry the onions in the extra-virgin olive oil for about 15 minutes until they smell lovely and have turned a golden colour (keep an eye on them so they don't burn). Season with salt, remove from the frying pan with a slotted spoon and set aside.

Put the matzah meal in a large bowl. Pour over the warm water and add a big splash of olive oil, a generous seasoning of salt and pepper, and the stock powder. Mix with your hands or a spoon. Let the mixture stand for 30 minutes.

After 30 minutes, add the eggs, schmaltz and fried onions to the bowl. Now 'mix it good', as my grandmother would say. At this point, the mixture will feel quite wet; that is fine, it should feel this way. Mix the ingredients together until everything is well combined, then taste it. Does it taste delicious? Schmaltzy, peppery, salty, oniony? Add more seasoning if you think it needs it, then cover the bowl and let it stand for an hour or more. You can even leave it in the fridge overnight.

To roll the matzah balls, bring a very large saucepan of water to the boil and season with salt.

Once the water is boiling, begin rolling the mixture into walnut-sized balls between your palms, dropping them into the water as you go. Continue until you have rolled all of the mixture into balls – if your pot isn't big enough to fit them all, cook them in two batches. When all of the balls have floated to the surface of the water, they are cooked. At this point you can leave the matzah balls in the cooking water over a very low heat for up to 30 minutes.

Place two balls in each bowl and cover them with chicken soup (page 102). Serve as described in the previous recipe, with poached carrots and sprigs of fresh dill and celery.

Note: When the matzah balls are cooked, my family usually leave them in the saucepan of water on a very low heat to keep them warm, or we put them in strained chicken soup that is warming on a low heat on the stove until we are ready to eat – but we don't leave them like this for more than half an hour, or they get soggy.

Lamb cutlets with pan sauce

It may seem simple to some, but lamb, specifically lamb cutlets marinated in cumin, paprika and good olive oil, is the meal I love most. Served with a salsa verde (page 141) – in this case a combination of fresh parsley, garlic, capers, good olive oil and vinegar – I love it even more. The herbaceous sauce is also delicious poured over boiled potatoes served beside the lamb.

In this recipe extra flavour is provided by making a second sauce with the juices from the meat. There is so much savouriness left in the pan after searing the lamb that it would be sad to leave it sitting there without a purpose. To make the most of those leftover juices and the brown bits stuck to the pan, you mix them with white wine, chicken stock and a splash of lemon juice to create a bright, emulsified sauce for pouring over the cutlets too.

SERVES 4

12 lamb cutlets, fat left on
(the thicker the cutlet the better)

2 tablespoons extra-virgin olive oil

MARINADE

1 teaspoon sweet paprika

1 teaspoon ground cumin

½ teaspoon freshly
ground black pepper

120 ml (4 fl oz) extra-virgin olive oil

2 tablespoons soy sauce

1 teaspoon honey

4 garlic cloves, lightly smashed
with the back of a knife

2 bay leaves, rubbed between your
fingers to release the flavour

To make the marinade and prepare the cutlets

Mix the ingredients for the marinade together in a small bowl. Place the cutlets in a tray and pour the marinade over them, then massage the marinade into the cutlets and leave them to rest in the marinade for at least 2 hours or overnight.

To cook the cutlets

Take the cutlets out of the fridge 30 minutes before you want to cook them.

Heat the 2 tablespoons of olive oil in a heavy-based or cast-iron frying pan over a medium–high heat, making sure there is enough oil to cover the bottom of the pan. When the oil is extremely hot (the surface will shimmer slightly), put the cutlets in the pan in a single layer without touching. Reserve the marinade and set aside.

Sear the cutlets for 2 minutes on one side, then turn them and sear the other side for 2 minutes. Press the sides of the cutlets into the pan to sear them too. Be careful not to overcook the lamb – you want to end up with blush pink meat, and it should feel soft when you press it. Take the cutlets out of the pan and leave them to rest on a chopping board for 5 minutes. Reserve the pan juices in the pan.

PAN SAUCE

30 ml (1 fl oz/⅛ cup) white wine

60 ml (2 fl oz/¼ cup)
Chicken stock (page 228)

1 teaspoon lemon juice (optional)

Salsa verde (page 141) to serve

To make the pan sauce and serve

While the cutlets are resting, make the pan sauce. Over a very low heat, pour the reserved marinade (including the garlic and bay leaves) into the frying pan with the lamb juices and bring the sauce to a gentle simmer for 1 minute. Pour in the wine to deglaze the pan, and using a wooden spoon scrape any browned bits stuck to the pan into the sauce. Add the chicken stock and gently simmer until the sauce has thickened slightly and is full of flavour, about 5 minutes, tasting it and seasoning with salt if needed. Add a teaspoon or so of lemon juice to balance the acidity, if required. Take the sauce off the heat and strain it to remove the aromatics.

Slice the meat on each cutlet away from the bone and cut into slices 1.5 cm (½ in) thick. Plate the cutlets by laying the pieces back together against the bone so that each cutlet resembles the same shape as before you sliced it. Spoon the pan sauce over the cutlets and serve straight away with the salsa verde.

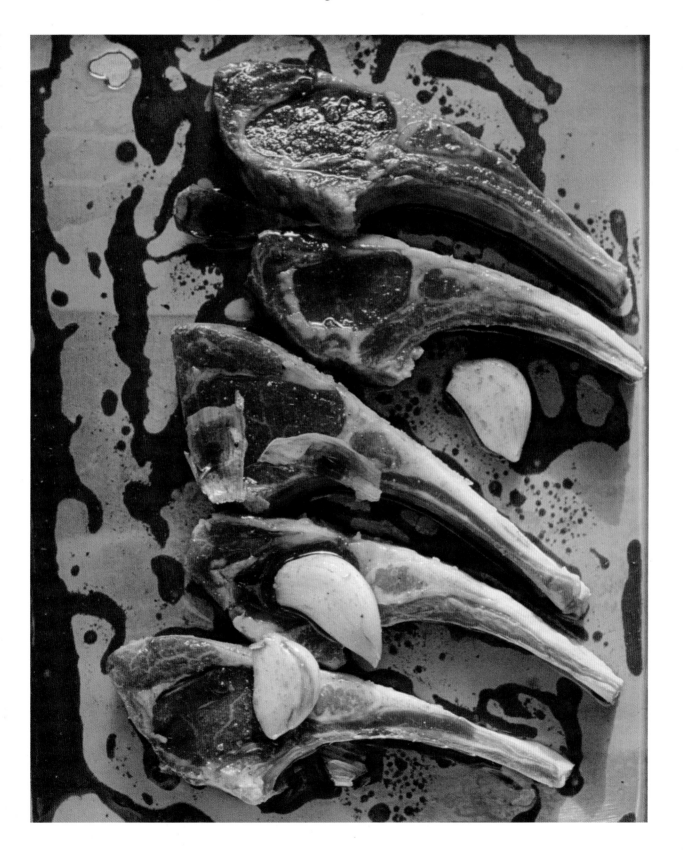

Minced lamb kebabs with zhoug, cumin oil and pickled red onion

North African Jews have a culture of outdoor grilling in the yard and barbecuing on balconies – we call the occasion as well as the grill itself a mangal. The culture of the mangal stems from the Sephardim cooking this way in Arabian homes of times past, in places where the weather was mostly good and so there were outdoor ovens and grills where communal cooking took place. Skewered meats, offal and minced meat were the foundation of such meals. I have learnt through reading Claudia Roden's *The Book of Jewish Food* that when they lived in Morocco, Jews would further season the kebabs at the table, putting out small bowls of chopped onion, parsley and ground cumin for people to pass around. Zhoug – a chilli relish that originated in Yemen – cheeks of lemon, toasted cumin oil, pickled red onions and warmed bread are a play on that tradition and have become a necessary addition at my table.

SERVES 4

KEBABS

500 g (1 lb 2 oz) minced (ground) lamb, with a good amount of fat (I ask for 80% meat, 20% fat)

1 onion, finely chopped

1 tablespoon extra-virgin olive oil

1 teaspoon ground cumin

1 teaspoon paprika

¼ teaspoon cayenne pepper

15 g (½ oz/½ cup) chopped flat-leaf (Italian) parsley (you don't need to be precious about picking the leaves, there can be some stalk in there)

25 g (1 oz/½ cup) chopped coriander (cilantro) (can include some stalks)

1 teaspoon freshly ground black pepper

2 teaspoons flaky salt

lemon cheeks to serve

To make the kebabs

Put all of the ingredients except for the lemon cheeks in a bowl and combine with clean hands until the mixture looks almost like a paste and holds together (squeeze it into a small ball – it should stay whole and not break apart).

To make skewered kebabs, divide the mixture into balls weighing roughly 60 g (2 oz) each. Holding a ball of minced meat in the palm of one hand, push a wide flat-bladed metal skewer onto the ball and then press the mixture over and around the skewer. Repeat for the remaining balls.

To make diamond-shaped kebabs, divide the mixture into balls each weighing roughly 45 g (1½ oz). Mould them between your palms into a diamond shape like a footy or rugby ball.

ZHOUG

½ bunch coriander (cilantro), roots cut off but stems kept, washed well

½ bunch flat-leaf (Italian) parsley, leaves roughly picked, washed well

3 green chillies, medium-hot variety

3 garlic cloves, crushed

1 teaspoon caraway seeds

seeds of 4 cardamom pods

100 g (3½ oz) sesame seeds, toasted until fragrant and golden in a dry pan

½ teaspoon salt

¼ teaspoon black pepper

75 ml (2½ fl oz) mild extra-virgin olive oil

PICKLED RED ONION

1 red onion, sliced in half, then finely sliced into half moons

white-wine vinegar

water

ice

CUMIN OIL

¾ cup ground cumin

250 ml (8½ fl oz/1 cup) extra-virgin olive oil

1 teaspoon salt

1 tablespoon white-wine vinegar

To make the zhoug

Put all of the ingredients except the olive oil in a food processor and blitz until well chopped. Pour the blitzed ingredients into a bowl and slowly fold through the olive oil until the mixture forms a rough paste. Store the zhoug in the fridge like this until needed; it should keep for a couple of weeks or more.

To make the pickled red onion

Place the red onions in a bowl and cover them completely with a ratio of ¾ white wine vinegar, ¼ cold water and a handful of ice. Leave to marinate in the fridge for at least an hour before serving.

To make the cumin oil

Toast the ground cumin in a dry frying pan over a very low heat until the spice smells fragrant, about 1–2 minutes, keeping an eye on it as it can easily burn. Turn off the heat, pour over the olive oil, season with the salt and stir to combine. After about 10 minutes, once the oil has cooled slightly, pour in the vinegar, stir and let it sit for at least half an hour before serving.

To cook and serve

To cook in a pan, coat a cast-iron or heavy-based frying pan with olive oil over a medium–high heat. When the oil is hot, working in batches cook the kebabs for about 6 minutes all up, turning them constantly so that each side gets a nice sear.

To cook over a charcoal fire, put the kebabs on an oiled grill that sits about 10 cm (4 in) above the glowing embers.

Serve the kebabs with the zhoug and small bowls of cumin oil and pickled red onion for people to pass around and spoon over the kebabs themselves.

Note: I like serving this dish with a couple of loaves of the Sesame focaccia flatbread (page 68) or rice and a tomato salad. You can also serve the kebabs with pickled whole green chillies, marinated capsicums (page 17) charred spring onion (page 115), pickled radish and turnips (page 229), charred eggplant (page 23), and labneh (page 224).

Minute steak with allium sauce

A straightforward plate. Steak seasoned with flaky salt, freshly ground black pepper and good olive oil. Spring onion tops blanched and turned into a pungent sauce made richer with the ever umami colatura di alici. And spring onion bottoms seared in the steak's juices to layer between the two. I think the emerald green sauce adds welcome character to the plate, and if I were cooking this for you I would make sure there were some Crisp vegetables with lemon vinaigrette (page 29) and possibly even a chunk of Sesame focaccia flatbread (page 68) to go with it.

This recipe makes quite a bit of allium sauce. Use the leftovers in salad dressings, or spoon it over roasted or boiled potatoes, roast chicken or a fillet of baked fish. It's also delicious mixed through shredded chicken to make a juicy sandwich filling. I love spooning it over a boiled egg and topping it with anchovies as a filling snack.

SERVES 2

4 pieces of very good quality, thinly cut minute steak

60 ml (2 fl oz/¼ cup) extra-virgin olive oil

ALLIUM SAUCE

3 tablespoons extra-virgin olive oil, plus 60 ml (2 fl oz/¼ cup)

4 garlic cloves, finely sliced

2 teaspoons colatura di alici (or 4 finely chopped anchovy fillets)

1 bunch spring onions (scallions)

60 ml (2 fl oz/¼ cup) water

grated zest of 1 lemon

1 tablespoon lemon juice

1 tablespoon Chardonnay vinegar

lemon juice to serve

To prepare the steaks and spring onions

Put the steaks on a tray and season with a big pinch of flaky salt (about 1 teaspoon per steak) and a little less freshly ground black pepper. Drizzle over 1 tablespoon of olive oil per steak and massage the oil and seasonings in. Let the steaks marinate for at least half an hour, covered, at room temperature.

Chop the bright green tops off the spring onions, then slice them in half and set aside. Trim the roots off the bottom halves of the spring onions and discard them, then set the bottoms aside for later.

To make the allium sauce

Heat a tablespoon of olive oil in a small saucepan over a low heat, and sauté the garlic until just golden, for about a minute, but don't take it any further otherwise you risk it burning. Add the colatura di alici or anchovies and cook gently for about a minute (if you are using anchovy fillets, stir them around the pan until they have melted into the oil). Add the green spring onion tops to the pan along with the water. Cover the pan with a lid, turn the heat up slightly, and simmer for 5–6 minutes until the greens are tender and the water has evaporated.

Transfer the mixture to a food processor, and add a tablespoon of water and 2 tablespoons of the olive oil. Blitz until smooth and a vibrant green colour. Add the lemon zest and juice, the vinegar, a big pinch of flaky salt, a small pinch of black pepper and the 60 ml (2 fl oz/¼ cup) of the olive oil and blitz. If the mixture is not coming together, add another splash of water to help move it around. Taste and check for seasoning and acidity. Add a bit more lemon juice to brighten the flavour if required, along with salt if it needs a further hit.

To cook the steaks and serve

Heat about 2 tablespoons of the olive oil in a heavy-based or cast-iron frying pan over a high heat. When the oil is extremely hot and almost smoking (be patient), sear the steaks in batches for about 40 seconds on each side and divide between two serving plates. Throw the spring onion bottoms in the pan and fry, turning them over every few seconds to lightly char on all sides, about 3 minutes all up.

To serve, spoon the allium sauce over the steaks, put the charred spring onions on top and season with flaky salt.

Note: Colatura di alici is an Italian-style fermented fish sauce that is stocked at specialty Mediterranean delis.

Moroccan Rosh Hashanah lamb with prunes, apricots and honey

In this dish, known as mrouzia in Morocco, lamb is browned and cooked slowly with sautéed onions, toasted spices and a handful of prunes and apricots under a cartouche of baking paper, as if you are tucking it in for a short nap. The result is a pot of very soft lamb, almost sweet from the dried fruit and coated in a thick, deeply spiced sauce. I remember eating this as a child on Rosh Hashanah (Jewish New Year), as the honey and fruit in the dish symbolise a sweet new year. You can make the dish with smaller chunks of lamb, or if like me you like the drama of serving a whole shoulder, buy the best quality cut and serve it in its entirety. I think this dish may be even better after a rest, the flavours having had time to relax deeper into both the meat and sauce.

SERVES 6

2.5 kg (5½ lb) lamb shoulder, off the bone (ask your butcher to keep the bones)

5 tablespoons extra-virgin olive oil

2 onions, finely chopped

8 garlic cloves, finely chopped

1 tablespoon minced ginger

2 cinnamon sticks

2 tablespoons ground coriander

1 tablespoon bahārāt

2 teaspoons ground turmeric

½ teaspoon allspice

juice of ½ lemon

375 ml (12½ fl oz/ 1½ cups) red wine

500 ml (17 fl oz/2 cups) Chicken stock (page 228)

2 tablespoons honey

200 g (7 oz) pitted prunes

200 g (7 oz) dried apricots

Look over the lamb shoulder and if there are any gristly bits, trim them off. Season the lamb shoulder generously with salt (about 2–3 tablespoons), a few big grinds of black pepper and about 60 ml (2 fl oz/¼ cup) of the olive oil. Rub this all over the lamb. You can leave the lamb to rest overnight in the fridge at this point if you want to let the flavours set in, but it is not essential if you are in a rush.

If the lamb has rested overnight, take it out of the fridge at least half an hour before cooking to bring the shoulder to room temperature.

Warm a tablespoon of the olive oil in a heavy-based flameproof casserole dish, then brown the lamb shoulder on all sides over a medium–high heat. Make sure the dish is big enough that the shoulder can lie open and flat so it browns evenly.

Remove the browned lamb from the dish and set aside. Sear the leftover lamb bones, then set them aside as well.

Add the onions to the casserole dish and sauté over a medium heat until they are golden, about 2 minutes. Add the garlic and ginger and cook for another 2 minutes. Add the spices to the onion mixture and stir so that they toast and become fragrant.

Add the lemon juice and deglaze at a gentle simmer, using a wooden spoon to loosen and scrape up any bits caught on the bottom of the dish. Pour in the red wine and let it whoosh up, then stir and bring to a fast simmer.

Nestle the lamb shoulder into the casserole dish, folding it back into the shape it was before it was deboned. Put the bones into the braising liquid too. Pour in the chicken stock and the honey, and bring the liquid back to a fast simmer, then reduce to a low heat. Cover with baking paper that is cut into a circle slightly bigger than the circumference of the pot, tucking in the edges. This will really help to seal in the steam. Cover with a lid and keep at a soft simmer for an hour.

After an hour, add the prunes and apricots and turn the lamb so that the other side is immersed in the liquid. Cover the dish with the baking paper and lid, and keep simmering over a low heat for another 2 hours or until the meat is very tender. If it looks dry at any point, pour in a little more stock or water.

By the end of the braise, the meat should be incredibly soft but still holding its shape, and sweet and almost sticky from the prunes and apricots. Taste the braising liquid towards the end of the cooking time (my mum and I usually check a couple of times to get the right balance). Sometimes it can be too salty or not sweet enough. If it tastes too salty, add a little more water, another small handful of apricots and a tablespoon or so of honey and simmer further until the fruit has broken down and soaked up some of the salt.

Serve the lamb and all its thick sweet juice straight away, or leave it to rest, and then carefully reheat before serving.

My aunty's couscous with vegetables, chickpeas and vegetable broth

I wrote this recipe down while talking with my aunties after we had just eaten a couscous feast with the family. My dad hadn't seen his aunty and cousins in years and nor had we. A large platter of couscous covered with chickpeas and vegetables caramelised in their own sweet juices was carried out from the kitchen, bringing with it a quick rush of fragrant steam. Everyone perked up – we could feel the presence of precious jewels – and I felt some sense of our shared past, of the importance of family and connection. To me North African couscous-based meals are about celebration and sharing, because in my family they have been made by someone who has treated the grains and vegetables with care and love. There is often meat too, and the meal is served with extra broth to pour over individual plates. It is magic. Prepare and eat slowly.

SERVES 4

VEGETABLE BROTH
AND CHICKPEAS

440 g (15½ oz/2 cups)
dried chickpeas

½ teaspoon bicarbonate
of soda (baking soda)

3 tablespoons extra-virgin olive oil

1 leek, roughly chopped

2 onions, roughly chopped

2 carrots, roughly chopped

4 celery stalks, roughly chopped

2 bay leaves

1 tablespoon peppercorns

1 cardamom pod

1 star anise

¼ teaspoon ground nutmeg

1 teaspoon ground turmeric

2 litres (68 fl oz/8 cups) water

To make the vegetable broth and cook the chickpeas

Put the chickpeas in a wide, deep bowl, cover with water, sprinkle with the bicarbonate of soda and leave to soak overnight.

If you have a couscoussier, use the bottom chamber of the set for these next steps; otherwise, use a heavy-based stockpot. Pour the extra-virgin olive oil into the pot over a medium heat and add the leek, onions, carrots and celery, followed by the bay leaves and peppercorns. Slowly sweat the vegetables over a low heat until they are just cooked and smelling sweet, about 15 minutes.

Add the cardamon, star anise, nutmeg, turmeric and a generous pinch of salt and pepper to the pot, stir and then cover the vegetables with the water. Bring to the boil, then reduce to a simmer and cook gently for about 2–3 hours. Skim off any foam on the top of the broth, and taste and season with more salt and pepper along the way if needed.

Strain the broth, discarding the cooked vegetables, and return the broth to the pot. Add the strained chickpeas, bring to the boil, then reduce the heat and simmer for about 15 minutes until they are tender but still slightly firm. Once ready, use a sieve or slotted spoon to take the cooked chickpeas out of the broth and set them aside. The rest of the hot broth will be used in the steps that follow.

To make the vegetables and couscous

Pour 2 tablespoons of the olive oil into another large, heavy-based saucepan and add three-quarters of the onions in a layer across the bottom. Pour over the cooked chickpeas, then sprinkle with half a teaspoon of sugar, 1 teaspoon of cinnamon, 1 teaspoon of flaky salt, a quarter teaspoon of black pepper and a generous glug (about 2 tablespoons) of olive oil.

VEGETABLES

140 ml (4½ fl oz) <u>extra-virgin olive oil</u>, plus extra for drizzling

3 <u>onions</u>, finely chopped

1 teaspoon <u>sugar</u>

2½ teaspoons ground <u>cinnamon</u>

2 teaspoons <u>flaky salt</u>

½ teaspoon freshly ground <u>black pepper</u>

half a <u>pumpkin (winter squash)</u>, such as <u>kent</u> or <u>butternut</u>, peeled, seeds and fibres scraped off and cut into 3 cm (1¼ in) wide wedges

2 <u>orange sweet potatoes</u>, peeled, sliced into 3 cm (1¼ in) wide rounds

2 medium <u>carrots</u>, peeled, sliced in half lengthways, then on an angle into 2.5 cm (1 in) wide pieces

3 small <u>white zucchini (courgettes)</u>, sliced lengthways

4 <u>shallots</u>, sliced in half

COUSCOUS

500 g (1 lb 2 oz) <u>dried couscous grain</u> (not precooked)

2 tablespoons <u>extra-virgin olive oil</u>

1¾ teaspoons <u>salt</u>

<u>plain yoghurt</u> to serve

Next, make another layer with the vegetables. Put the vegetables, including the shallots, on top of the onion and chickpeas, cover the vegetables with the rest of the onion and then sprinkle over another half a teaspoon of sugar, 1 teaspoon of cinnamon, 1 teaspoon of flaky salt, a quarter teaspoon of black pepper and a generous glug (about 2 tablespoons) of extra-virgin olive oil.

Pour 500 ml (17 fl oz/2 cups) of the hot broth over the vegetables, along with a tablespoon of olive oil – you want the vegetables to shine. Keep the rest of the broth warm to serve with the couscous. Cover the vegetables with a sheet of baking paper, tucking the edges down the sides of the pot as if tucking them to sleep – this cartouche traps steam and prevents condensation affecting the vegetables. Cover the pot with its lid and cook at a gentle simmer over a low–medium heat for 30 minutes.

While the vegetables are cooking, rinse the couscous well under running water twice before tipping it into a bowl. Season the couscous with half a teaspoon of salt.

When the vegetables have been cooking for half an hour, remove the cartouche and set aside. Pour the washed couscous into the steaming basket of the couscoussier and set it on top of the pot of vegetables (make sure there is enough stock in the pot of vegetables to create steam). If you don't have a couscoussier, use a standard steaming basket or metal colander with small holes that will fit snugly over the heavy-based pot you are using.

Dip your fingers into the couscous to create a few big holes that will allow the steam to come through, then cover with a lid and steam for 15 minutes.

Take the couscous off the heat and cover the pot of vegetables with the cartouche and lid to continue cooking. Put the couscous in a large bowl and pour over 500 ml (17 fl oz/2 cups) of water. Stir the couscous to help the grains absorb the water. Once the couscous has cooled a little, pour over the 2 tablespoons of olive oil and season with 1 teaspoon of the salt, then rub everything into the couscous with your hands, spreading the grain evenly, until the water and oil has been absorbed. (The reason we steam the couscous first is so that the grain can more easily absorb the water and oil.)

Pour the couscous back into the steaming basket, remove the lid and cartouche from the pot and set the couscous over the vegetables again. Cover and leave to steam for 10 minutes. Discard the cartouche.

Preheat the oven to 245°C (475°F).

Take the couscous and vegetables off the heat, returning the lid to the pot to keep the vegetables warm. Season the couscous further with the remaining three-quarter teaspoon of salt or to your liking (keep in mind that the vegetables and soup are already well seasoned so the couscous doesn't need to be super salty), mix and taste. Keep the couscous covered and warm until the vegetables are ready.

Remove the lid from the pot of vegetables: at this stage they should be soft and cooked through. Pour over a generous drizzle of olive oil and sprinkle over the remaining half a teaspoon of cinnamon. Place the pot, uncovered, in the oven for 10 minutes, until the vegetables are golden and the sauce has thickened slightly.

To serve

To prepare the couscous for serving, pour a few ladles of the broth over the couscous to moisten it, rubbing it in using your hands or a wooden spoon, then put it onto a serving plate and shape it into a mountain. Arrange the vegetables down the sides of the couscous, and bring it and the remaining broth to the table. To serve, place some couscous on each plate, top with the vegetables and chickpeas, then spoon over some more of the soup. If you feel like it, you can drop a spoonful of plain yoghurt on top, as my dad often enjoys doing.

Note: I have purposely made this recipe vegetarian, with a vegetable-based broth. If you are inclined towards a meat version, add a couple of chicken carcasses and/or beef bones and stewing meat to the broth. Serve the meat with the vegetables and couscous.

Summer tomato, onion and pecorino crostata

When I can get my hands on true, sun-drenched summer tomatoes I want to do as little to them as possible before eating them. Vine-ripened and warmed by the summer sun, all they need is slicing with a sharp knife, and then a big glug of extra-virgin olive oil, a sprinkle of flaky salt and a few young basil leaves. I also love cosying up fresh cheese like ricotta beside the tomato; a quartered piece of stone fruit might make its way onto the plate too. Another way to turn really good tomatoes into a meal is to make this flaky crostata. Onions are cooked down until they are a caramel colour before being hidden under a layer of jewel-like summer tomatoes. Lots of black pepper, olive oil, flaky salt and fresh oregano, thyme and basil are scattered and drizzled over the top. Serve with a crisp salad on the side and some wine, for a light and cool meal under the hot summer sun.

MAKES ONE CROSTATA
TO SERVE 4–5

DOUGH

250 g (9 oz) plain (all-purpose) flour

50 g (1¾ oz) pecorino, finely grated

125 g (4½ oz) unsalted
butter, chilled and diced

75 ml (2½ fl oz) iced water mixed
with 1 teaspoon apple-cider vinegar

FILLING

2 tablespoons butter

1 tablespoon extra-virgin olive
oil plus extra for drizzling

3 onions, sliced in half
then finely sliced

20 g (¾ oz) pecorino

4 medium–large summer
tomatoes and a handful of
smaller cherry/baby tomatoes
(preferably a variety of colours)

3 oregano sprigs

3 thyme sprigs

1 egg

1 sprig fresh young basil for serving

To begin making the filling

Heat the butter and olive oil in a heavy-based or cast-iron saucepan over a low heat. Add the onions, season with a generous pinch of salt and stir, then leave them to cook slowly for about an hour until they are very soft and caramelised. Be patient; let them go slowly until golden. When they are done, leave to cool completely.

Cut the larger tomatoes into slices 1–2 cm (½–¾ in) thick, and the smaller tomatoes into halves or thirds.

To make the dough

Combine the flour, pecorino and a pinch of salt in a bowl. Add the chilled butter, then rub the flour and butter together with your fingertips until the cubes of butter are the size of baby peas and the mixture resembles coarse breadcrumbs. Add enough of the iced water and vinegar to just bring the mixture together to form a dough (don't overwork it). If the dough is dry, add more water a tablespoon at a time, but be careful that it doesn't get too sticky. Cover the dough, then leave it to rest in the fridge for at least 1 hour, or ideally overnight.

To construct and bake the crostata

Preheat the oven to 220°C (430°F).

Roll out the chilled pastry into a rough circle that is about 30 cm (12 in) in diameter. As you roll it out, you will notice big chunks of butter throughout the dough – that is perfect, because those chunks will give the pastry a flaky, crisp texture. Line a baking tray with baking paper, then put the rolled-out pastry onto it.

Leaving a border about 5 cm (2 in) around the edge, spread the cooled onions in a thin layer over the pastry. Shave a light layer of pecorino over the onions, then lay over the tomatoes, overlapping them slightly and grouping them together based on the tomato variety. Season the tomatoes with flaky salt and a few grinds of black pepper. Pour over a glug of extra-virgin olive oil, then sprinkle a few sprigs of oregano and thyme over the tomatoes.

Gently fold the edges of the pastry up over the tomatoes, overlapping and crimping the pastry as you work your way around. If by this time the dough has warmed up and feels limp, put the crostata in the fridge to cool down and harden for 15 minutes (this will ensure a flaky pastry).

Beat the egg in a bowl, then paint the pastry with the egg wash. Bake the crostata for 20–30 minutes, until the pastry is crisp and golden. Let it cool slightly before serving with fresh young basil over the top.

On tasting and seasoning
throughout the cooking process

A while ago I was watching a friend who is a chef cook a simple soup. It was a plain moment, nothing super special – he probably doesn't even remember it – but it was a moment that has stuck with me. As we were talking I noticed how good the kitchen was beginning to smell. I had of course learnt about the importance of salt before, but it was as he was seasoning the onions and green chilli that I truly learnt about layering vegetables with salt and fat. I don't know why it was that moment in particular that grounded in me the importance of seasoning, but nevertheless it was a lesson that has stuck. It was a realisation that what he was making was so simple in its essence, but it was his attention to seasoning every step of the way, right from the start, that created the most flavourful base possible for the rest of the soup.

Seasoning a dish throughout the cooking process may seem like a simple lesson, but it is everything: it results in a more rounded final dish, one that you have gotten to know deeply, every step of the cooking way. Through reading Claudia Roden and Rachel Roddy, and through eating my mother's food, I have learnt about the importance of trusting yourself and allowing yourself a certain freedom when it comes to food and cooking. Don't be too strict; learn the history of the dish you are cooking and follow a recipe, yes, but taste, taste, taste the whole way and be flexible. Layer flavour and adjust the seasonings to suit you.

When I wrote many of the recipes in this book I struggled to quantify the amount of salt and pepper, and the level of acidity in a dish. For me seasoning is deeply personal and I believe in trusting your own tastebuds. I think getting to know how much salt and acid your food needs is a skill you can hone. Follow my recipe for kebabs, then roll a small amount between your hands and fry it off in a pan. Taste it to see if your tastebuds are asking for something more – maybe a little more salt, a handful more parsley, or does it actually need a touch of lemon to balance out the fat? Taste everything before fully cooking it and look for a good balance between acidity and rich fat. Learn what you like and don't like, and season accordingly.

Vegetables

Sugarloaf cabbage with stracciatella and anchovy emulsion 134
String beans with lemon and dijon dressing 135

Parmesan rinds

Parmesan broth with borlotti beans and salsa verde 140
Fennel braised in parmesan broth 143

Braised beluga lentils with marinated silverbeet 144
Spring vegetables and toasted buckwheat with vinaigrette 146
Dressed soft lettuce salad 149

Ways with artichokes

Boiled artichokes with vinaigrette 152
Stuffed artichoke bottoms with onion and pea sauce 155
Roman-Jewish-style fried artichokes 156

No matter the amount of prep that I need to get through, opening the crates of produce when I arrive at the restaurant never feels like a chore. Each morning of service, my kitchen team and I are met at the front door of the restaurant by a stack of crates full of vegetables and fruits. Depending on the season, there may be crates overflowing with leafy greens, fat pods of broad (fava) beans, sweet bulbs of baby fennel and radishes that look like big rubies. A whole crate of oranges for the bar to slice into drinks and for the kitchen to poach for chocolate cake, look beautiful in their abundance: the ordinary charm of fresh produce.

When it comes to buying vegetables, you want the very best you can get your hands on. Give them a gentle squeeze and a sniff, and check with the grocer that they were grown locally and are in season. Without wanting to sound like a purist, I have come to realise that I most enjoy eating and cooking carefully produced, in-season vegetables. M.F.K. Fisher's writings have guided my understanding of the best ways to prepare vegetables and how little cooking they require when they are young, in season and fresh. You need only sauté them briefly in good olive oil or even sweet butter to be able to enjoy their natural juices. They are perfectly delicious served like this, or you can marinate them if you feel like giving them a little extra love. A splash of vermouth vinegar with the olive oil, and maybe also the addition of a fresh bay leaf rubbed between your fingers to the pan will deepen the vegetables' natural flavours. Another way I like cooking vegetables is to gently braise them with some sort of stock to bring out their sweetness. I take a bulb of fennel, slice it into wedges and fry it for a minute before braising it in a simple parmesan broth until the stock has mostly reduced, resulting in tender, sweet segments of fennel (page 143). For a little caramelisation and texture, I grate a wedge of Parmigiano Reggiano over the fennel before giving it a final bake in the oven.

During spring I love poaching baby leeks no thicker than my thumb and serving them with grilled asparagus, toasted buckwheat and a dijon vinaigrette (page 146). If broad beans or peas are in season, I make an effort to shuck and blanch them, and throw them over this dish as well – I encourage you to do the same. My family's favourite vegetable dish when they eat at the restaurant is my sugarloaf cabbage (page 134): sliced, grilled and smothered in an anchovy emulsion, the charred wedges sit on top of fresh stracciatella, a creamy cheese, making for decadent mouthfuls. The Braised beluga lentils with marinated silverbeet (page 144) go wonderfully nestled beside the tomato crostata (page 122), and the String beans with lemon and dijon dressing (page 135) are a delicate match for the salty Roast chicken with thyme, anchovy butter and potatoes (page 96). A wonderful partner for the luscious Lamb cutlets with pan sauce (page 106) is a bowl of soft lettuce leaves dressed in a tangy vinaigrette (page 149). Rapha's family have always done salads really well. These are not over-the-top, include-every-vegetable kinds of salad, but ones created in a rather more minimalist style. His family grow different kinds of lettuces, peas, cucumbers and herbs in their front garden, and fill the widest bowls they own with torn lettuce leaves, fresh peas and cucumbers, lots of lemon and olive oil drizzled over the top. The salad in this chapter was inspired by these big, fresh assemblages of lettuce.

With some focaccia or baguette on the side, and served with a tin of fish, a wedge of cheese, a quick tortilla or an omelette, most of these vegetable dishes can become a whole meal.

Sugarloaf cabbage with stracciatella and anchovy emulsion

I think one of the most delicious ways to eat cabbage is sliced into wedges that are cooked hard on a cast iron pan or over a grill. I love using sugarloaf cabbage for this dish, mostly because it has a beautiful shape but also for its slightly sweet, crispy texture. However, if you can't find sugarloaf, use regular cabbage instead.

SERVES 4 AS A STARTER OR SIDE

3 tablespoons extra-virgin olive oil plus extra for drizzling

1 sugarloaf cabbage, sliced into quarters (or half a small cabbage, cut into 3 wedges if you can't find sugarloaf)

1 cup stracciatella

Pangrattato (page 223)

ANCHOVY EMULSION

100 ml (3½ fl oz) extra-virgin olive oil

25 g (1 oz) garlic (about 6 cloves), finely sliced

60 g (2 oz) good quality salted anchovies

75 g (2¾ oz) unsalted butter, diced and softened

½ teaspoon finely ground black pepper

To make the anchovy emulsion

Heat the oil in a small saucepan over a low–medium heat. Add the garlic and anchovies, and nudge the anchovies around the pan using a wooden spoon until they melt and the garlic is golden and fragrant, about 2–3 minutes. When the mixture is an oily, glossy paste, take the pan off the heat and whisk in the butter cube by cube until it melts and the mixture emulsifies. Season with the pepper and set aside covered to keep the emulsion warm and at a loose consistency.

To cook the cabbage

Preheat the oven to 200°C (390°F). Heat a generous amount of the olive oil (enough to cover the base) in an ovenproof heavy-based or cast-iron frying pan over a high heat. When the oil is hot, sear the cut sides of the cabbage quarters for about 2 minutes per side. Once the quarters have a nice golden sear on each side and the cabbage has softened a little, gently flip and sear the uncut side for about 2 minutes or until the exterior is nicely charred and has softened.

Take the pan off the heat and transfer the cabbage halves to a plate or chopping board. Using a pastry brush, liberally spread the anchovy emulsion over the cut side of the cabbage, working it between the layers as well so that the emulsion is evenly spread throughout each half (you may not need to use all of it). Return the cabbage to the pan and put it in the oven for 5–10 minutes or until the kitchen smells of fragrant garlic and caramelised anchovy.

To serve

When I serve this at the restaurant I plate one quarter per dish. These instructions follow that method but you can also serve all the cabbage quarters on one big platter. For individual plates, drop a big dollop of the stracciatella onto each serving plate and make an indentation with the back of a spoon in which the cabbage will sit. Lay one of the charred quarters over the stracciatella, sprinkle with a handful of pangrattato, season lightly with flaky salt and drizzle with a glug of olive oil. Repeat with the rest of the cabbage quarters and serve straight away.

String beans with lemon and dijon dressing

Dressed in a dijon, soy and lemon rind dressing, this is a delightful salad of green and yellow beans.
It is light and by extension uplifting, the soy adding a subtle saltiness that penetrates the vegetables.
I love lightly cooking string beans so they still taste slightly raw after you have blanched and shocked them
in ice. I slice the beans into two different shapes for texture: fine ribbons and thin round coins. However,
if you don't have the time or patience to do this, feel free to slice all of the beans into fine strips.

SERVES 4 AS A SIDE

350 g (12½ oz) string beans,
(ideally a mix of yellow and green)

LEMON RIND PURÉE

3 lemons

¼ teaspoon sugar

45 ml (1½ fl oz) grapeseed oil

45 ml (1½ fl oz) extra-virgin olive oil

DRESSING

1 tablespoon lemon juice

½ teaspoon dijon mustard

1 teaspoon soy sauce

80 ml (2½ fl oz/⅓ cup)
extra-virgin olive oil

To prepare the beans

Bring a saucepan of water to the boil, seasoning it well with salt. Blanch
half of the beans for 30 seconds, or until they are just cooked but still
have bite to them, then shock them in iced water for 20 seconds, then
remove and set aside. Repeat this process with the remaining beans.

Using a very sharp knife, slice half of the beans into long thin pieces
that resemble fine ribbons. Slice the other half of the beans into round
pieces about 5 mm (¼ in) long.

To make the lemon rind purée

Bring a small saucepan of water to the boil. Peel the rinds off the
lemons with a sharp knife and blanch them in boiling water for
30 seconds, then shock them in iced water for 30 seconds. Repeat this
process four more times; this will reduce the bitterness of the rind.

Blitz the rinds, sugar, grapeseed oil and olive oil in a strong food
processor or blender until almost smooth. Strain the mixture through
a sieve into a small bowl – keep the juices that fall into the bowl and
discard the solids left in the sieve.

To make the dressing

Whisk the lemon juice, dijon mustard and soy sauce into the bowl
with the lemon rind juices. Slowly whisk in enough olive oil to create
a sturdy dressing. Season to taste with a pinch of flaky salt and freshly
ground black pepper.

To serve

Put the beans in a bowl and pour over the dressing. With clean hands,
toss the beans and dressing together with a pinch of flaky salt until the
dressing covers every strand and slice of bean.

Parmesan rinds

Some years ago I learnt to hang on to my parmesan rinds. There is too much flavour in them to waste. As the rinds sit and steep in stocks, broths and ragus, they begin to soften, imparting a rich savoury flavour. Save the rinds in a little box in your fridge to pull out and use at the right moment. The two recipes that follow make use of a deeply flavoured parmesan broth in different ways.

SALAME TIPO
SECONDIGLIANO
PICCANTE

€ 24,00 al kg

PARMIGIANO
REGGIANO
€ 29,00 al kg

CORALLINA
di VISSO
€ 24,00

Parmesan broth with borlotti beans and salsa verde

I have a crush on borlotti beans. They are the beans that catch my eye, a legume I can't look past when they begin to make their appearance on market shelves. Their slender, speckled pink pods are too beautiful; it would be strange not to grab a paper bag full of them and bring them back to the kitchen – I am sure you will feel the same. Simmering the borlotti gently in a broth spiked with parmesan rinds transforms them from their raw, unseasoned state into tender, full-flavoured morsels. When they're served in a bowl full of the broth that they were cooked in, topped with a confident drop of green sauce (better known as salsa verde), you will have to stop yourself from overeating them. If you have any leftover beans, they are delicious eaten with barbecued lamb or spooned over grilled focaccia and some ricotta salata shaved over the top.

SERVES 4

BROTH

2 onions

1 leek, white part only
(but save the tops)

1 celery stalk

200 g (7 oz) button mushrooms

40 g (1½ oz) unsalted butter

2 tablespoons extra-virgin olive oil, plus extra for cooking

½ garlic bulb (slice a bulb in half horizontally)

125 ml (4 fl oz/½ cup) white wine

about 4 parmesan rinds saved from your parmesan wedges

2 litres (68 fl oz/8 cups) water

3 thyme sprigs

2 bay leaves

1 tablespoon peppercorns

To make the broth

Chop the vegetables into a rough, small dice.

Over a medium heat, melt the butter and extra-virgin olive oil in a large heavy-based or cast-iron saucepan or stockpot. Add the onion, leek, celery, mushrooms and garlic and stir. Cook the vegetables for about 20 minutes, until they are golden brown and smell delicious. Season with salt and pepper.

Splash in the white wine and leave it to bubble up and cook off for 2 minutes.

Add the parmesan rinds and a generous glug of olive oil to the pot. Cover the rinds and vegetables with the water. Add the thyme, bay leaves and peppercorns, and bring to the boil. Reduce the heat a little, cover slightly and leave the broth to simmer gently for about an hour and a half, by which time it should have a deep savoury taste.

BEANS

500 g (1 lb 2 oz) fresh borlotti beans in their shells, weighing 200 g (7 oz) when podded

½ garlic bulb (slice a bulb in half horizontally)

1 tomato, sliced in half

½ red chilli

3 oregano sprigs

60 ml (2 fl oz/¼ cup) extra-virgin olive oil

SALSA VERDE

½ bunch flat-leaf (Italian) parsley

1 tarragon sprig

½ oregano sprig

2 teaspoons capers, rinsed and squeezed dry

1 garlic clove

1 tablespoon red-wine vinegar

60 ml (2 fl oz/¼ cup) extra-virgin olive oil

parmesan to serve (optional)

To cook the beans

Strain the stock and clean the pot. Pour the clear broth back into the pot. Pick the borlotti beans from their pods and put them in the broth along with the garlic, tomato, chilli, oregano, extra-virgin olive oil and season with flaky salt and a few grinds of black pepper (the soup should taste well seasoned to penetrate the beans as they cook). Simmer for 30–40 minutes, or until the beans are tender but not mushy.

To make the salsa verde and serve

Pick, wash, and then dry the herbs. Roughly chop the capers. Mash the garlic with flaky salt, then mix with the herbs, capers, vinegar and olive oil in a bowl. Season with flaky salt and freshly ground black pepper.

Serve the broth in bowls, with a ladleful of borlotti beans and a confident drop of salsa verde on top. Season with a little more flaky salt and pepper if needed and another glug of olive oil. You can also shave over some parmesan if desired.

Fennel braised in parmesan broth

When fennel is fried in some olive oil, then gently braised in parmesan broth until most of the liquid has reduced, you are left with very tender, almost caramelised wedges. I love dusting these just-cooked pieces of fennel with more parmesan, and then baking them until golden, the cheese becoming a little crisp in the process. Like a lot of my recipes that are quite rich, a squeeze of lemon juice over the top rounds everything out at the end. This fennel is delicious with fish or lamb, or served with braised beluga lentils (page 144), fresh ricotta and bread.

SERVES 4 AS A SIDE

4 bulbs baby fennel, with stalks

2 tablespoons extra-virgin olive oil, plus extra for drizzling

250 ml (8½ fl oz/1 cup) Parmesan broth (page 140)

20 g (¾ oz) parmesan

½ lemon

Prepare the fennel by trimming off the fennel stalks (save them to use in a vegetable stock and save the fronds for the garnish). Peel off any unappealing outer layers, then wash. Halve the fennel lengthways, then cut each half through the core into thirds.

Preheat the oven to 220°C (430°F).

Heat the extra-virgin olive oil in a deep ovenproof frying pan over a medium heat. When the oil is hot, add the fennel wedges to the pan, being careful not to overcrowd it. Season with flaky salt and fry the fennel for 5 minutes on each side, or until a golden caramel colour, then pour over the stock or broth until it comes halfway up the fennel. Increase the heat a little to bring to a gentle simmer. Cook the fennel for about 10 minutes, until the stock has reduced a little and the wedges are just tender but still have some bite: when you insert a fork into the fennel, you want it to have a little bit of resistance.

Grate the parmesan directly over the fennel, season with freshly ground black pepper and drizzle over some olive oil (if you have any leftover parmesan rinds from making the parmesan broth, tuck them into the pan too). Put the pan in the oven and bake for about 8–10 minutes, until the fennel is tender and golden, and the parmesan is browned and crisp. Squeeze the lemon over the fennel, garnish with the fronds and serve immediately.

Braised beluga lentils with marinated silverbeet

Tiny black beluga lentils look like caviar, hence the name. I like them because they hold their shape and still have an al dente bite to them once cooked. Here the brothy lentils are mixed with silverbeet that has been blanched and marinated while still warm, allowing the vinegars and olive oil to seep into the leaves.

SERVES 4

MARINATED SILVERBEET

500 g (1 lb 2 oz) silverbeet
(Swiss chard)

½ shallot, peeled and sliced
into very fine strips

pulp of 2 tomatoes (keep the
flesh for the lentil braise)

1 teaspoon sherry vinegar

1 teaspoon lemon juice

3 teaspoons red-wine vinegar

80 ml (2½ fl oz/⅓ cup)
extra-virgin olive oil

BRAISED LENTILS

180 g (6¼ oz/1 cup)
baby beluga lentils

2 tablespoons extra-virgin olive oil

1 onion, finely chopped

2 celery stalks, finely chopped

1 carrot, finely chopped

½ bulb fennel, finely chopped

3 flat-leaf (Italian) parsley
sprigs, finely chopped

15 g (½ oz) unsalted butter

1 bay leaf

750 ml (25½ fl oz/3 cups)
Chicken stock (page 228) or
Vegetable stock (page 227)

To make the marinated silverbeet

Roughly chop the silverbeet into 4 cm (1½ inch) pieces, discarding any woody stalks as you go. Blanch the leaves in boiling water for about 2 minutes, then set aside in a bowl.

Mix together all the ingredients for the marinade and pour it over the warm leaves. Toss the leaves and marinade together, then leave the silverbeet to steep in the marinade for at least 10 minutes.

To braise the lentils

Rinse the lentils under cold running water until the water runs clear, and pick out any debris such as pebbles. Set aside.

Heat the olive oil in a wide frying pan over a low heat. Add the chopped vegetables and season with a big pinch of flaky salt and freshly ground black pepper, then sweat the vegetables until softened, about 10 minutes.

Add the parsley, reserved tomato skins and butter, and let it sizzle for a minute before adding the rinsed lentils. Stir thoroughly until the lentils are glossy and toasted, about a minute.

Add the bay leaf and the stock, and bring to the boil, then leave to simmer gently over a low heat partially covered, until the lentils are tender but not mushy, about 20–25 minutes. Check on the lentils from time to time to make sure they are not sticking to the bottom of the pan or drying out. When the lentils are cooked, there should be a small amount of broth left in the pan. If the lentils are still hard or are dry by this time, add more stock or water as needed and simmer until tender. Taste and season further with salt and pepper.

To serve

Put the brothy lentils in a bowl, and top with the silverbeet, a few spoonfuls of the leftover marinade and a generous glug of olive oil. Mix well, taste and season to your liking with salt and pepper, then serve nestled beside fish, chicken or lamb. This is also a delicious accompaniment to the Fennel braised in parmesan broth (page 143).

Spring vegetables and toasted buckwheat with vinaigrette

A small bundle of poached baby leeks, silky and slender. Seasonal asparagus spears lie beside the leeks, glistening with olive oil and still crisp after a brief sear in a hot pan. The vinaigrette, loose and fragrant, falls over the spring vegetables. This dish needs the toasted buckwheat and a good cheddar – both ingredients add a nutty taste and important texture. The soft herbs are also essential. Make this when you need a tangy vegetable side dish to accompany a rich, decadent main.

SERVES 4

60 ml (2 fl oz/¼ cup) extra-virgin olive oil, plus 2 tablespoons

50 g (1¾ oz) buckwheat

500–600 g (1 lb 2 oz–1 lb 5 oz) baby leeks (if you can't find baby leeks, substitute with normal leeks)

300 g (10½ oz) asparagus

65 g (2¼ oz) good quality manchego, broken into rough chunks

VINAIGRETTE

2 tablespoons dijon mustard

2 tablespoons apple-cider vinegar

1 teaspoon Chardonnay vinegar

20 g (¾ oz) shallot, finely chopped

80 ml (2½ fl oz/⅓ cup) extra-virgin olive oil

handful of chervil, leaves roughly picked

3 tarragon sprigs, leaves roughly picked

3 tablespoons water

To make the vinaigrette

Whisk the dijon, both vinegars and shallots in a bowl until combined. Keep whisking and very slowly pour in the extra-virgin olive oil. When all of the oil is whisked in, very gently chop the chervil leaves into a rough heap, and do the same with the tarragon leaves. Set aside a small amount of the soft herbs for garnish and stir the remainder into the vinaigrette. Whisk in the water to loosen the dressing, then season to taste with flaky salt and freshly ground black pepper. The vinaigrette should taste tangy and sharp with a bit of spice from the mustard and shallots, but it should be balanced by the sweet cider vinegar and fruity Chardonnay vinegar. If it is too tangy, balance the flavour by adding a little more of the sweet vinegar.

To toast the buckwheat and cook the vegetables

Heat 60 ml (2 fl oz/¼ cup) of the olive oil in a frying pan over a low heat and toast the buckwheat until it is golden brown and crisp – it will taste almost like popcorn when it is ready and it will soak up quite a bit of the oil. Keep an eye on it, as it can burn easily. Set the toasted buckwheat aside to cool on a plate.

Slice the dark green tops off the leeks (either discard them or save for a stock), then clean the leeks very well under running water to remove all dirt. Bring a saucepan of well-salted water to the boil, then poach the leeks for about 6–8 minutes, until they are soft but don't fall apart when you insert a knife into them (if you are using normal leeks, cook them for about 10–12 minutes). Transfer them to a bowl of iced water and shock until the leeks are cool, about 2 minutes, then slice them in half lengthways (if using normal leeks, slice them lengthways into quarters). Set aside.

Cut about 3 cm (1¼ in) off the bottom of each asparagus spear and discard (these bits are usually woody and tough), then slice the asparagus in half. Heat another 2 tablespoons of the olive oil in the frying pan over a medium–high heat, and sear the asparagus very briefly so that they stay firm but gain some colour, taking care not to overcook them as they will become floppy. Season the cooked asparagus lightly with flaky salt and set aside.

To serve

Put the leeks on a platter and season lightly with flaky salt. Spoon over some of the vinaigrette so as to partially cover the leeks. Lay the asparagus on top of the leeks on one side, season with flaky salt and spoon a little of the vinaigrette over them too (you may not need to use all of the vinaigrette; save the rest to use on salads, boiled eggs and so on). Scatter the manchego on top of the leeks on the opposite side to the asparagus. Sprinkle the reserved chervil and tarragon over the vegetables, then spoon over the toasted buckwheat and a little bit of the fragrant olive oil it was fried in to serve.

Dressed soft lettuce salad

Don't look past this salad – its simplicity is what makes it striking. The main drawcard is the thick dressing, so tangy yet sweet. Although he would think it is a ridiculous thing to say, Rapha is very good at salad dressings. He has always been able to perfectly balance the garlic, honey, vinegars, mustard and oils. This dressing is a collaboration between us. My ratios were completely off until Rapha tested it and fixed a couple of issues. Fresh, crisp salad is a joy to eat, so fill your biggest platter with the torn leaves of a couple of different lettuce varieties (I use baby gem and butterhead lettuces, but feel free to choose the lettuce variety you like best), throw over some soft herbs like tarragon and chervil, and some fresh peas and cucumber too, then drizzle with the dressing, giving it all a good toss until every leaf is coated.

DRESSING MAKES ENOUGH FOR ABOUT 3 SALADS

1 red <u>baby gem lettuce</u>

1 green <u>butterhead lettuce</u>

soft herbs like <u>tarragon</u> and <u>chervil</u>, (optional)

40 g (1½ oz/¼ cup) <u>fresh peas</u>, shelled

2 <u>Lebanese (short) cucumbers</u>, peeled, sliced in half lengthways, then each piece sliced on the diagonal into rough 5 cm (2 in) pieces

DRESSING

2 <u>garlic cloves</u>

1 tablespoon <u>dijon mustard</u>

60 ml (2 fl oz/¼ cup) <u>red-wine vinegar</u>

60 ml (2 fl oz/¼ cup) <u>white-wine vinegar</u>

1 teaspoon <u>honey</u>

250 ml (8½ fl oz/1 cup) <u>extra-virgin olive oil</u>

60 ml (2 fl oz/¼ cup) <u>water</u>

To make the dressing in a blender or food processor

Blitz the garlic, dijon, vinegars, honey, extra-virgin olive oil, a big pinch of flaky salt and a few grinds of black pepper in the blender or food processor until fully combined. If you are using a food processor, pour in the water with the motor running; if you are using a blender, add the water 1 tablespoon at a time, blending between each addition to combine.

To make the dressing by hand

In a bowl, whisk the garlic, dijon, vinegars, honey, a big pinch of flaky salt and a few grinds of black pepper until combined, then slowly pour in the extra-virgin olive oil in a steady stream while continuing to whisk. When all of the oil has been incorporated, pour in the water in a steady stream and whisk continuously until combined.

Taste to check that the flavours are balanced between the acid, salt and garlic. This shouldn't be a garlic-heavy or very vinegary dressing, so if either of these flavours are dominant, adjust the ingredients as necessary: for example, add more oil or water if it is too vinegary, or a little more garlic if you can't taste it at all, and so on.

To serve

Pick the leaves from both lettuces and wash and dry them thoroughly. Leave the smaller gem lettuce leaves whole but tear the larger leaves in half. Put all of the lettuce in a salad bowl together with your chosen herbs, peas and cucumber. Drizzle with about 140 ml (4½ fl oz) of the dressing and toss to coat. Serve straight away.

Ways with artichokes

Artichokes hold a hazy nostalgia for me. I remember as a kid sitting with my dad in my grandparents' kitchen. In my memory it is a sepia-coloured room.

The table was round and faced a small courtyard where naana (mint) and louiza (lemon verbena) bushes were growing for making tea. Trinkets, plastic table coverings, old photos and art from their past lives in Morocco and Israel-Palestine filled the room. A silver pot containing boiled artichokes and lemon sat on the table and beside it was a plate of poached beef tongue with peas, lemon, olive oil and broth. My dad showed me how to peel back the leaves to reach the heart of the artichoke. Every leaf we tore through with our teeth meant we were closer to the main prize: the soft artichoke heart. It was an unfussy, comforting meal, one that for me centred on the artichoke and its tender, meaty petals.

When it comes to eating artichokes, my dad is adamant. 'You need to know how to eat artichokes. You need to know. People don't eat them right and this upsets me because they leave most of the artichoke full. My god, what a waste! You have to put the whole petal in your mouth and scrape the whole length with your teeth,' he says, while miming the action of tearing into an artichoke petal. 'This is what it is all about, the artichoke. And the best part of it is the heart.' He almost weeps as he says this. 'I peel off the hairy middle and pick the edible part up and eat the whole thing. So yum.'

The artichoke is native to North Africa and the Mediterranean, and many Jewish cultures have taken to the prickly flower. Here I provide three ways that I like to prepare them.

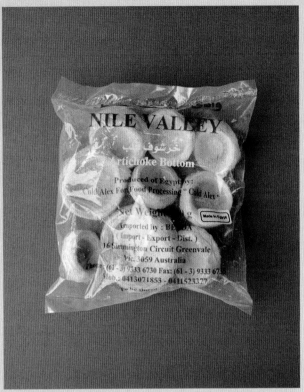

Boiled artichokes with vinaigrette

This first recipe is perhaps the most straightforward way to prepare an artichoke: simply boiled and served with a vinaigrette to dip the leaves into. It's how my grandfather used to make them, so will always remain a favourite way to eat them.

SERVES 3 AS INDIVIDUAL
SERVES OR 6 IF SHARING

2 lemons

3 fresh globe artichokes

extra-virgin olive oil for drizzling

VINAIGRETTE:

35 g (1¼ oz) dijon mustard

15 ml (½ fl oz) white-wine vinegar

5 ml (⅛ fl oz) Chardonnay vinegar

80 ml (2½ fl oz/ ⅓ cup) extra-virgin olive oil

1½ tablespoons water

To make the vinaigrette

Whisk the dijon and both vinegars in a bowl until combined, then very slowly pour in the olive oil while whisking continuously. When all the oil is combined, pour the water into the vinaigrette and whisk to loosen the dressing. Taste and season with flaky salt and freshly ground black pepper. The tang and acidity of the vinaigrette should be balanced by the sweetness of the vinegars.

To prepare and boil the artichokes

Juice one of the lemons and set aside with the juiced halves for later. Slice the other lemon into cheeks.

Peel away any small, woody leaves at the base of an artichoke, then use kitchen scissors to cut off the little thorns on the outer leaves. Cut off most of the stem, leaving 2 cm (¾ in) of it attached, then use a vegetable peeler to peel away its tough outside layer. Slice 4 cm (1½ in) off the top of the artichoke to create a flat surface and discard the cut-off leaves. Rub a lemon cheek all over the cut parts of the artichoke to stop it oxidising. Repeat this process with the remaining artichokes and lemon cheeks.

Put the cleaned and trimmed artichokes stems up in a wide saucepan, cover with water and season well with fine sea salt. Add the lemon juice and the juiced halves to the water along with the lemon cheeks. Bring the water to a gentle boil over a medium heat and leave the artichokes to cook for 30–35 minutes, until tender and soft but not falling apart. Check them at 30 minutes by pulling off a leaf and testing it: if the flesh is soft and meaty when you pull at the leaf with your teeth, then the artichokes are ready.

To serve

Shock the artichokes in a bowl of iced water for 2 minutes until cool. Put the artichokes on a plate and gently pull at the outer leaves to open them out a little so they look nice. Serve the artichokes at room temperature seasoned with flaky salt, a drizzle of extra-virgin olive oil and a bowl of the vinaigrette for people to dip the leaves into.

Stuffed artichoke bottoms with onion and pea sauce

For this dish the artichoke bottoms are stuffed with meat and braised in a sauce fragrant with onions and peas. This is a traditional Sephardic recipe and the way we eat them in my dad's family.

SERVES 4–5

1 lemon

2 x 500 g (1 lb 2 oz) bags frozen artichoke bottoms

1 piece of day old bread

500 g (1 lb 2 oz) minced (ground) lamb (80% lean meat, 20% fat)

3 garlic cloves, crushed

½ teaspoon ground coriander

1 teaspoon onion powder

1 teaspoon ground cumin

½ teaspoon allspice

1 tablespoon bahārāt

7 g (¼ oz/¼ cup) finely chopped flat-leaf (Italian) parsley

about 1½ teaspoon salt

2 teaspoons freshly ground black pepper

1 teaspoon extra-virgin olive oil

ONION AND PEA SAUCE

6 large onions, finely chopped (at least 530 g/1 lb 3 oz once chopped)

60 ml (2 fl oz/¼ cup) extra-virgin olive oil

1 teaspoon salt

¼ teaspoon freshly ground black pepper

½ teaspoon ground cinnamon

½ teaspoon ground turmeric

250 ml (8 fl oz/1 cup) water

juice of ½ lemon

250 g (9 oz) peas (fresh or frozen)

To prepare the artichokes

Put the artichoke bottoms in a big bowl and cover them with hot water until they soften, then drain and set aside.

To make the onion and pea sauce

Sauté the onions in 3 tablespoons of the olive oil in a large heavy-based or cast-iron saucepan with a tight-fitting lid over a low–medium heat, cooking for about 20 minutes until the onions have softened and turned a rich, golden caramel colour. Add the salt, pepper, cinnamon, turmeric and half a cup of the water, then stir and simmer covered for a further 5 or so minutes. By now the onions should have collapsed into a rich jam-like sauce. Keep over a very low heat or turn the heat off until the filled artichokes are ready to be put into the sauce.

To make the meat stuffing

Tear the bread into small pieces, put them in a large bowl and sprinkle with a tablespoon of water, then leave for 5 minutes until the bread has absorbed the water. Add the meat, garlic, spices, parsley, salt, pepper and olive oil and work into a soft paste with your hands. Roll a small ball between your palms and sear it quickly in a frying pan to taste and check for seasoning. After tasting, season further with more salt and pepper to your liking.

To stuff and cook the artichoke bottoms, and serve

Hold an artichoke bottom in your palm, grab about 35 g (1¼ oz) of the meat and press it into the centre of the bottom, shaping the mixture so it sits like a plump mound within the artichoke. Nestle the filled artichoke into the onion sauce. Repeat with the rest of the artichoke bottoms. If you have leftover meat, roll it into balls and place them around the artichokes.

Mix the remaining half a cup of water with the lemon juice and pour it over the artichokes and onion sauce. Add half the quantity of the peas. Cover with the tight-fitting lid and cook at a gentle simmer over a low heat for about 20 minutes. Uncover the pot, sprinkle over the remaining half of the peas and cook for a further 10 minutes without the lid. If the sauce looks dry at any point, add a splash more water. Serve with rice or couscous.

Roman-Jewish-style fried artichokes

Finally, there are artichokes prepared in the classic Roman-Jewish way, a recipe that famously originates from the old ghettos of Rome. For this dish, the artichoke is fried into a crispy flower and served with a cheek of lemon.

<u>SERVES 4 AS A STARTER</u>

2 <u>lemons</u>, plus cheeks to serve

8 large <u>globe artichokes</u> or
16 <u>baby artichokes</u>

<u>extra-virgin olive oil</u> for frying

<u>To prepare the artichokes</u>

Slice the 2 lemons into quarters and squeeze them into a large bowl of cold water (reserve the lemon quarters for rubbing). Trim the artichokes by removing and discarding layer after layer of the dark green outer leaves to expose the very fine, light-green and yellow leaves within. These are the edible leaves.

Using a paring knife, cut off the top half of the artichoke. The idea is to leave the tender, edible lower portion of the artichoke leaves intact, while removing the tough, thorny tops. Now cut off most of the artichoke stem, leaving about 6 cm (2½ in) of stem attached. Peel away the tough, outer layer of the stem and cut off and discard any tough, dark green skin on the outside of the artichoke heart. Go slowly and carefully. As you peel, rub a quarter of lemon over the artichoke – this will help it retain its colour by preventing oxidisation.

If you are using baby artichokes, or artichokes which are thorn free, the artichoke will be ready to cook at this point. If you have larger artichokes with fuzzy but sharp chokes in the centre, scoop them out with a spoon. If it is too difficult to remove the choke at this point, do so after the first fry, when the leaves have softened.

Put each peeled and trimmed artichoke in the bowl of lemon water as you finish trimming them.

<u>To fry into crisp little flowers and serve</u>

Take the artichokes out of the lemon water and dry them well. In a large saucepan, heat 3 cm (1¼ in) of olive oil over a medium–high heat. When the oil is quite hot, add the artichokes – you should see steady yet not intense streams of bubbles rising around the artichokes. Fry for about 10 minutes, until they are tender enough that you can pierce the thickest part with a skewer. Adjust the heat as needed to maintain steady streams of bubbles around the artichokes. If the oil doesn't completely cover the artichokes, turn them frequently with a skewer so that all sides touch the oil at some stage.

Using a slotted spoon, transfer the artichokes to a plate lined with paper towels to drain. When cool enough to handle, gently pull open each leaf until each artichoke begins to look like an open flower.

If you didn't remove the choke before, now is the time to scoop out and discard it.

Increase the heat to high and return the artichokes to the oil for no more than 5 minutes, turning them frequently, until browned and crisp.

Transfer them to a plate to drain on fresh paper towels. Season with flaky salt and serve straight away, hot off the kitchen bench alongside cheeks of lemon for friends and family to liberally squeeze over the flowers.

Pasta Plates

Handmade pasta

Fresh egg pasta 166
Fresh cavatelli pasta 169

Spaghetti with whipped anchovy butter, garlic and chilli 170
Linguine with capers, bottarga and lemon 173
Spaghetti with confit cherry tomato and fennel seeds 174
Spaghetti with clams in garlic and chilli 176
Conchiglioni with braised leek and cavolo nero green sauce 180
Cavatelli with squid and XO sauce 185
Pappardelle with broad beans, peas and veal ragu 186
Paccheri with tuna and guanciale amatriciana 188
Tagliatelle with prawns and nduja pangrattato 192

I think, in a way, making dough runs in my blood. My safta on my mother's side is naturally excellent at making dough from scratch and turning it into various savoury and sweet pastries and breads, like Rugelach (a pastry filled with chocolate or jam, page 208) and the bread called challah (page 72). I have grown up watching my safta's and my mother's hands knead and roll dough, sometimes together, sometimes apart. My great grandmother, a Holocaust survivor, used to make her own pasta dough for lokshen, a traditional Jewish egg noodle eaten with chicken soup. My safta has told me how she used to watch her mother hang the noodles over a broom to dry.

My dad's side of the family, is also good with dough, making filo pastry for cigars (spiced minced lamb wrapped in a filo cigar and deep fried) and sweet doughs for things like Raiff (a traditional Moroccan tea biscuit, page 205). Fresh egg pasta dough is one of the doughs I have always wanted to get right. I have been pretty intense about it at times, my main desire being to create a pasta that has a good bite. A soft, floppy strand of pasta won't do (although I think there is a time and place for it – for example, the soft lokshen in chicken soup).

By no means am I an expert pasta chef. But the handmade egg pasta recipe in this chapter has been my go-to – making a versatile strand of pasta with character and bite. It is the product of hours of testing. The low hydration of the dough means that it takes time to work and even more time to laminate and roll. I used to make hundreds of portions of it each week for lockdown pasta packages in Melbourne. At one point I thought my wrist would give in from the intense kneading. But don't let this story discourage you (and probably don't make a hundred portions of this at once like I did). Pour yourself a glass of wine and enjoy the process, laminating and rolling until you end up with a tray full of fresh golden pasta that you can toss through a silky sauce. The second pasta recipe is egg free, and because it is made from just durum wheat semolina and water, it is quite quick to bring together.

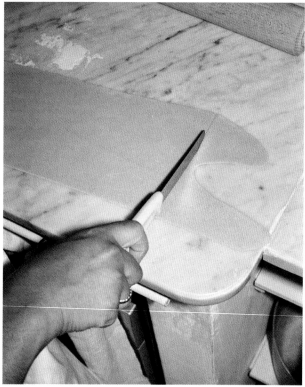

After a few minutes of kneading, and then shaping the dough into small cavatelli on a wooden gnocchi board, you will be rewarded with a chewy bowl of pasta with craggy little ridges to soak up the sauce.

Which brings me to cooking and tossing pasta. Always salt your pasta water once it has come to a gentle boil. Taste the water and make sure that it tastes well seasoned – not so salty that you recoil but salty enough that the water isn't bland. I usually season with about 3 tablespoons of salt per 1.25 litres (42 fl oz/5 cups) of water. When the time has come for the cooked pasta to meet the sauce, a big splash of starchy pasta water, oil or fat and a good energetic toss are everything, the point of the latter being the emulsification of the starch and fat – it's this that creates a silky sauce. Because every recipe is different, the amount of pasta water required will vary. That being said, no matter the sauce you are making, have a small ladle at the ready and once the pasta is cooked and you've transferred it to the frying pan, ladle some of the starchy water over the pasta and sauce. Make sure you are using a light pan, one that is big enough to hold the pasta and sauce with room to move. You must be able to easily toss the pasta in the pan, either by giving the pan a few shakes up and down to flip the pasta, or by tossing the pasta energetically using tongs. This step is essential.

Pasta can be a simple weeknight meal, and there are recipes for that in this chapter, but I think a bowl of pasta can be so much more than that. By turning on the lamp in your kitchen and opening a good bottle of wine, the same bowl of Spaghetti with whipped anchovy butter, garlic and chilli (page 170) that you make for an easy post-work dinner can turn into a romantic bowl of pasta that you cook for a crush on the weekend.

This chapter features a number of pasta plates I have put on the menu at Hope St – luscious, vegetable-forward pasta plates and seafood-rich pastas – as well as some of my favourite pastas to make when I have people over. Many of these pastas are inspired by the time I spent in Italy, eating, talking and taking notes on the Mediterranean.

Handmade pasta

Making pasta with your hands: this is a process that takes time, love and being okay with making a bit of a mess. Inviting friends over to join you in the slightly laborious pasta making process is a good idea. The two pasta doughs that follow are purposely quite dry, and as such take more kneading to come together than some other pasta doughs, requiring your effort and energy. A drier dough will give you pasta with texture, which I prefer – I don't often want to eat a soggy noodle (unless it is angel hair pasta in chicken soup). If a pasta dough is too hydrated the result is a loose strand of pasta without much bite. Don't let this extra effort turn you off – the reward for your hard-worked hands will be fresh pasta with a silky texture and an al dente bite, perfect for tossing into a luscious sauce.

Fresh egg pasta

I like a sturdy strand of pasta. To create this, a sheet of dough, deep yellow in colour, pressed into itself and laminated multiple times so that it comes out with texture and bite, is ideal. I then slice the sheet into ribbons, fold them through my fingers, dust them with more semola and leave them to dry. You can cut the sheets into thin strands for tagliatelle, wider ones for pappardelle, or even squares for fazzoletti, a handkerchief-shaped pasta. This is more or less the recipe we have been using at Hope St since we opened. The rich egg pasta pairs well with decadent sauces like the braised baby leek and cavolo nero (page 180), ragus such as the veal and broad bean (page 186), and luscious seafood sauces including the prawn and nduja (page 192) and clams with garlic and chilli (page 176).

SERVES 4–5

2 eggs (total weight 116 g/4 oz)

6 egg yolks (total weight 110 g/ 4 oz), with egg whites set aside

260 g (9 oz) tipo 00 pasta flour

100 g (3½ oz) semola rimacinata flour (durum wheat semolina), plus extra for dusting

To make the dough

Crack the eggs into a bowl, add the egg yolks and whisk.

Mix the flours in the bowl of an electric mixer fitted with a dough hook attachment. With the mixer set to a medium speed, slowly pour in the beaten eggs. Keep a close eye on the ingredients, making sure the egg is being evenly distributed through the flour. After about 2 minutes it will start forming a rough, shaggy dough. Knead the dough on a medium speed for another 3 minutes, then tip the dough out of the bowl and onto a clean surface, lightly dusted with some semola flour.

Knead with your hands by pushing the dough firmly away from you with the heel of one hand to stretch it, then folding it back on itself and rotating it a quarter turn. Put your other hand on top of the bottom one for extra strength. Repeating this action, knead for 10 minutes, until the dough has formed a tight ball and is smooth and leathery. If you are struggling to make the dough come together by hand, add a little bit of the leftover egg whites to lubricate it – this will make the dough easier to knead. Put the dough in a covered bowl and leave it to rest for at least 1 hour.

To roll the pasta

Lightly dust a few trays with semola flour. Divide the dough into eight balls of equal size.

Work with one piece of dough at a time, keeping the others covered with a tea towel to stop them from drying out. Roll out the first piece so that it is about 3 mm (⅛ in) thick.

Set the pasta roller to its widest setting and roll the dough through it three times.

Lay the sheet of dough flat. Take the right edge of the sheet and fold it into the middle, then fold the left side to cover the right and roll the dough through the widest setting again. Now roll this sheet through the same setting three more times.

Repeat the folding and rolling process twice more. If the dough is at all sticky as it goes through the pasta roller, dust both sides lightly with semola flour.

Set the pasta roller down a setting (so it is a little thinner) and repeat the whole process above until you get to the second-last setting on the pasta roller, then stop (I usually stop at setting 6 on my KitchenAid pasta roller).

Lay the now laminated sheet of dough over the back of a chair or on a bench to dry a little (check on it after 15 minutes and if it is drying out too quickly cover it with a tea towel).

Repeat this process with the remaining pieces of dough.

When all of the sheets of dough are slightly dry, cut the sheets in half and trim the uneven ends so they are straight, if you wish. If you have a pasta cutter attachment, run the sheets through the pasta roller to create strands. Otherwise, cut the dough lengthways into strips 2.5–3.5 cm (1–1½ in) wide to create pappardelle.

Lightly sprinkle the strands or strips in semola and leave to dry for a few minutes on the trays dusted with semola.

To cook the pasta

Cook the pasta in boiling salted water for 2–3 minutes, until it is al dente – you want it to retain some bite, so keep checking it so as not to overcook. Pull the pasta out of the water with tongs when it is ready and toss in a pan with your chosen sauce.

Note: If you don't have a freestanding electric mixer to knead the dough in the first stage, you can do it all by hand – it will just take more physical effort on your part. Why not share the kneading with a friend?

Fresh cavatelli pasta

SERVES 4–5

400 g (14 oz) semola rimacinata
(durum wheat semolina),
plus extra for dusting

200 ml (7 fl oz) lukewarm water

To make the dough

Put the semola flour in a large bowl. Slowly add the water, mixing with your hands to incorporate the liquid into the flour. When the water has been absorbed, use your hands to bring in the rest of the flour to create a shaggy dough. Continue working the dough until you have a messy ball, then turn it onto a clean bench lightly dusted with semola flour.

Begin the kneading process by pushing the dough firmly away from you with the heel of one hand to stretch it, then folding it back on itself and rotating it a quarter turn. Put your other hand on top of the bottom one for extra strength. Find a strong kneading rhythm, pressing down with your body weight as you go. If the dough feels too sticky at any point, dust with more flour. Work the dough this way for about 10–15 minutes until you have a smooth and elastic ball of dough.

Let the dough rest for at least 30 minutes, covered with a tea towel.

To roll the cavatelli

Divide the dough into six balls of equal size. Work with one ball of dough at a time, keeping the others covered to stop them from drying out. Using the palms of your hands, roll the first ball into a rope about 25–30 cm (10–12 in) long. Using a knife or a dough scraper, cut the rope into 2 cm × 5 cm (¾ in × 2 in) pieces. Then, one by one, press each piece against a gnocchi board or the back of a fork with your thumb, rolling it across the ribbed surface. Put each freshly rolled cavatelli on a floured tea towel or board to dry out (be careful not to let them touch) while you roll the other pieces of dough. Leave them out until they are completely dry to the touch, which might only take an hour or so, or you can leave them overnight.

To cook the cavatelli

Bring a saucepan of well-salted water to the boil, drop the cavatelli in and cook until they float to the surface – this should take 2–3 minutes. Then, using a sieve or a spider, pull the pasta from the water and toss it into a pan with a bit of pasta water and your chosen sauce.

Spaghetti with whipped anchovy butter, garlic and chilli

This is what I like eating when I am suddenly hungry and feel like something salty and luscious. It is kind of like aglio e olio, but the addition of the whipped anchovy butter takes it to a sultry place. As the butter and olive oil melt together and the garlic begins to smell fragrant, I wait patiently to be able to toss the pasta in. The strands of spaghetti become wet and silky from their toss in the pan with the pasta water and a glug of olive oil. The flicks of red chilli flakes and bright parsley gleam. This could be a dish you make spontaneously for a lover perched on a kitchen bench. It is rich but still honest and relaxed. I will sip on a glass of wine, or vermouth on ice, as I try to eat it slowly. Serve on simple plates, in a warm room.

SERVES 4

440 g (15½ oz) spaghetti

4 tablespoons Whipped anchovy butter (page 67)

60 ml (2 fl oz/¼ cup) extra-virgin olive oil

8 garlic cloves, finely sliced

pinch of chilli flakes

handful of flat-leaf (Italian) parsley, finely chopped (optional)

Bring a saucepan of water to the boil, season generously with fine sea salt, stir and then add the spaghetti.

While the pasta is cooking, warm the anchovy butter and olive oil in a wide frying pan over a medium heat until the butter has melted and is beginning to sizzle gently. Add the garlic, chilli flakes and a generous amount of freshly ground black pepper and nudge everything around the pan.

When the garlic smells fragrant and the butter is just starting to foam slightly, lift the pasta out of the water and drop it straight into the pan (if the pasta is not ready by the time the garlic is golden, turn off the pan and wait until the pasta is al dente before continuing). Throw over the parsley if you are using it, pour in a small ladle of the pasta water, shake the pan and stir everything energetically until each strand is coated in a silky sauce. If it seems dry, add another splash of the pasta water and stir to emulsify.

Taste and season further with flaky salt if needed. Serve straight away on simple plates and eat while hovering over the kitchen bench.

Linguine with capers, bottarga and lemon

This pasta comes together so quickly and feels like the perfect thing to eat outside in warm weather, or ideally to make and take to the beach to eat. The only stove time required is cooking the pasta and frying the garlic and capers – then all you have to do is toss the ingredients in a big bowl. The salty combination of capers and shaved bottarga mingling with lemon and fresh parsley gives this pasta a delightful, oceany feel. You really do need good extra-virgin olive oil for this recipe (something full flavoured and peppery) – because the sauce is so simple, using the best quality ingredients you can find is important.

SERVES 4

440 g (15½ oz) linguine

120 ml (4 fl oz) extra-virgin olive oil plus extra to serve

8 garlic cloves, finely chopped

50 g (1¾ oz/¼ cup) baby capers, rinsed and squeezed dry

grated zest of 2 lemons

¼ cup flat-leaf (Italian) parsley, roughly chopped

20 g (¾ oz) bottarga (dried mullet or tuna roe) plus extra to serve

Bring a saucepan of water to the boil, season generously with fine sea salt, stir and then add the linguine.

While the pasta is cooking, heat 60 ml (2 fl oz/¼ cup) of the olive oil in a frying pan over a low–medium heat and sauté the garlic until it is golden and fragrant, about a minute. Add the capers and sauté together until the capers crisp up a little.

When the pasta is cooked, lift it out of the water with tongs and put it in a bowl large enough to toss the linguine in (if the pasta is not ready by the time the capers are crispy, turn off the pan and wait until the pasta is al dente before continuing).

Pour the garlic, capers and residual cooking oil over the linguine, and scatter with the lemon zest and parsley. Shave over the bottarga, pour over the remaining olive oil, and ladle in 60 ml (2 fl oz/¼ cup) of pasta water. Season with flaky salt and a generous amount of freshly ground black pepper.

Toss the pasta by shaking the bowl energetically, forming waves in the air, or toss with the tongs or a wooden spoon to bring it all together. If the pasta is looking at all dry, add another glug of olive oil and a little more pasta water, and keep tossing until it looks glossy. Taste and season further, if you'd like.

Serve with more shaved bottarga over each individual plate and a little more extra-virgin olive oil over the top.

Spaghetti with confit cherry tomato and fennel seeds

This is a very good tomato sauce to coat strands of spaghetti or to toss with a pasta shape that catches the sauce, like rigatoni. The peak of summer is the perfect time to make it, when tomatoes are most flavoursome and you can find a mix of yellow, orange and red cherry or grape tomatoes at the market. The tomatoes and fennel seeds are nudged around the pan to extract their juices, the fennel seasoning the gently cooked tomatoes more than you would imagine. Once they have softened slightly, the tomatoes are covered in very good extra-virgin olive oil to create a confit, the garlic and chilli infusing into the oil too. The creaminess of the sauce comes from blending a third of the cooked tomatoes and returning them to the pan to mix with the rest of the sauce.

SERVES 2

60 ml (2 fl oz/¼ cup) extra-virgin olive oil, plus 125 ml (4 fl oz/½ cup) for simmering

8 garlic cloves, finely sliced

1 red chilli, finely sliced

1 teaspoon fennel seeds, crushed in a mortar and pestle

550 g (1 lb 3 oz) cherry/grape tomatoes (a mix of yellow, orange and red)

60 ml (2 fl oz/¼ cup) white wine

220 g (8 oz) spaghetti

10 g (¼ oz) grated parmesan plus remaining wedge to serve

basil leaves to garnish

To make the sauce

Heat the 60 ml (2 fl oz/¼ cup) of extra-virgin olive oil in a wide frying pan over a low–medium heat and sauté the garlic and chilli until the garlic is golden and fragrant, about 1–2 minutes. Season with the fennel seeds, half a teaspoon of flaky salt and a quarter teaspoon of freshly ground black pepper, and fry for a further minute until the seeds are toasted. Add the tomatoes and toss or nudge them around in the oil until each fruit glistens. Season further with half a teaspoon of flaky salt, stir and sauté for another minute.

Turn the heat up a little to medium, pour in the white wine and bring everything to a gentle simmer for 2 minutes until the alcohol has cooked off. Cover the tomatoes in olive oil (about 125 ml/4 fl oz/½ cup in my pan), then bring the tomatoes to a rapid simmer for 2 minutes.

Reduce the heat to very low so that the tomatoes are at a gentle simmer and there are small bubbles around them. Cook for about 25–30 minutes until the tomatoes have softened and the juices have collapsed into the pan.

Transfer one-third of the tomatoes in a bowl and use a hand-held blender to blitz them until creamy. Pour the blitzed tomatoes back into the frying pan and mix them with the whole baby tomatoes. Simmer gently for another 5 minutes, then season to taste with more salt and pepper. Turn off the heat and cover the sauce to keep warm.

To cook the pasta and serve

Bring a large saucepan of water to the boil over a high heat. Season well with salt (the water should taste well seasoned, but you should not recoil from salt overload), stir, then add the spaghetti and stir again.

Cook until the pasta is al dente, meaning that it is cooked through, but still has some bite to it (usually about 2 minutes less than the recommended cooking time listed on the packet).

Bring the pan of tomatoes back to a gentle simmer over a low heat. When the pasta is cooked, lift it out of the water using tongs and put it in the pan, along with 60 ml (2 fl oz/1/4 cup) of the pasta water and the parmesan. Stir energetically with the tongs or a wooden spoon to emulsify. Increase the heat to medium as you stir so that the sauce is at a steady simmer – you want to see bubbles forming around the side of the pan. If the pasta needs more sauce, add another 60 ml (2 fl oz/1/4 cup) of the pasta water and keep tossing until you have a silky sauce and the pasta is well covered. Serve straight away on warmed plates, garnished with basil. Bring the remaining wedge of parmesan to the table for people to grate over their plates if they wish.

Spaghetti with clams in garlic and chilli

My favourite sound in the kitchen is a bunch of clams hitting a hot pan of sizzling garlic and chilli – if you make only one recipe from this book, I think it should be this one. And you should make it again and again, until you have grown to know the dish very well and you know exactly how you like it. After you have cooked it multiple times, you can begin to add ingredients that make you happy, though you'll want to keep the additions simple so they don't distract from the clams, the main star. I like adding Italian greens but sometimes I will throw in a few cherry tomatoes, or a cup of white beans, or even a spoonful of nduja (page 26) to replace the fresh chilli. Whether you cook it in its pure form or with additions, this plate of pasta will bring you joy and satisfaction – and that is what a good recipe should do.

SERVES 2

1 kg (2 lb 3 oz) clams (vongole)

80 g (2¾ oz) Italian bitter greens, such as rapini (broccoli rabe) (optional)

220 g (8 oz) spaghetti

2 tablespoons extra-virgin olive oil

6 garlic cloves, finely sliced

1 red chilli, finely sliced

125 ml (4 fl oz/½ cup) white wine

handful of flat-leaf (Italian) parsley, roughly chopped, plus more to serve

15 g (½ oz) butter

To prepare the clams and bitter greens

Place the clams in a bowl, cover with cold water and leave them to soak for 30 minutes to remove any sand or dirt. Transfer the clams to a clean bowl, making sure you don't bring along any of the sand that has sunk to the bottom of the first bowl. Discard the sandy water and set the clams aside.

If including the bitter greens, pull the leafy part of the rapini away from the woody stem and discard the stem. Roughly chop or tear the rapini leaves into thin strips, keeping any florets, and set aside.

To cook the pasta

Bring a large saucepan of water to the boil over a high heat. Season with salt (but not too much, as the pasta sauce will be quite salty from the clam brine), stir, then add the spaghetti and stir again. Cook until the pasta is al dente, meaning that it is cooked through, but still has some bite to it (usually about 2 minutes less than the recommended cooking time listed on the packet).

To make the sauce and serve

While the pasta is cooking, heat the olive oil in a wide frying pan over a low heat and gently fry the garlic and chilli for about a minute. When the garlic is golden and fragrant, add the clams and pour in the wine, toss briefly and then cover with a lid, leaving it slightly open. Steam the clams until they pop open (this should take about 5 minutes). As each clam opens, take it out of the pan and put it on a plate to the side. If after 10 minutes any clams in the pan are not fully open, throw them out. Keep the clam sauce at a gentle simmer over a low–medium heat for 5 minutes and pick the clam meat from the shells, leaving a handful intact.

Pour 60 ml (2 fl oz/¼ cup) of the pasta water into the sauce and stir; the starch in the water will help thicken the sauce. Add the rapini greens, if using, to the sauce and bring to a gentle simmer for 2 minutes to reduce.

Add the parsley, butter, clam meat and the handful of clams in their shells, and stir quickly to melt the butter. Taste the sauce and season with flaky salt and plenty of freshly ground black pepper. By now the spaghetti should be cooked. Lift the pasta out of the water using tongs and put it directly into the pan, along with another 60 ml (2 fl oz/¼ cup) of the pasta water. Stir energetically with the tongs or a wooden spoon to emulsify. Keep the sauce at a steady simmer over a medium heat as you stir – you want to see bubbles forming around the sides of the pan. If the pasta needs more sauce, add another 60 ml (2 fl oz/¼ cup) of the pasta water and keep tossing until you have a silky sauce and the pasta is well covered. Serve straight away, with more chopped parsley on the side for people to scatter over their bowls.

Conchiglioni with braised leek and cavolo nero green sauce

<u>SERVES 4</u>

8 <u>garlic cloves</u>, peeled

<u>extra-virgin olive oil</u> to cover

350 g (12½ oz) <u>baby leeks</u>

120 g (4½ oz) <u>cavolo nero (Tuscan kale)</u>

75 g (2¾ oz) <u>butter</u>

60 ml (2 fl oz/¼ cup) <u>white wine</u>

2 <u>parmesan rinds</u> (optional)

2 tablespoons grated <u>Parmigiano Reggiano</u> or <u>Grana Padano</u>, plus extra for sprinkling

125 ml (4 fl oz/½ cup) <u>Vegetable stock</u> (page 227) or water

pinch of <u>chilli flakes</u>

440 g (15½ oz) <u>conchiglioni</u>

block of <u>parmesan</u> to serve

<u>To make the confit garlic</u>

In a small saucepan, cover the garlic cloves with olive oil (about 250 ml/8½ fl oz/1 cup) and add a pinch of salt. Very gently simmer the garlic over a low heat for about 10 minutes, until the cloves are soft and golden brown, then turn off the heat and leave to cool. The garlic can keep like this, under oil, for up to a month in the fridge.

<u>To braise the leeks and make the sauce</u>

Prepare each leek by cutting away its outer layer and discarding it. Slice the leeks down the middle lengthways to open them up, then slice them in half crossways and wash each thoroughly, as they are usually quite dirty inside.

Next pick the cavolo nero leaves, discarding the woody branches, and roughly chop them (you will want to have no more than 100 g/3½ oz of leaves). Bring a saucepan of salted water to the boil and blanch the leaves for 2–4 minutes, until just cooked.

In a deep sauté pan or casserole dish with a lid, pour 60 ml (2 fl oz/¼ cup) of the oil from the confit garlic into the pan along with the butter and warm over a medium heat. Melt the fats gently, then add the leeks and stir. Cook gently for 5 minutes, then pour in the wine and let everything sizzle gently for 2 minutes until the alcohol has cooked off, but there is still liquid in the pan. Season with 2 teaspoons of flaky salt and a few grinds of black pepper. Throw in a couple of parmesan rinds, if you have them.

Heavily butter a piece of baking paper big enough to fit over the pan, then place it on top of the leeks, carefully tucking the edges of the paper in and under the leeks to create a cartouche. This will trap the steam, keeping all the cooking juices in the pot rather than letting them evaporate. Put the lid on the pan as well, and reduce the heat to low. Leave the leeks to stew over a low heat for about 15 minutes.

Remove the cartouche from the leeks and stir – by now the leeks should have collapsed and caramelised, and have an almost silky texture. Remove the parmesan rinds and turn the heat off.

Put the cavolo nero, parmesan, vegetable stock or water and chilli flakes in a food processor, together with 8 cloves of the confit garlic, 60 ml (2 fl oz/¼ cup) of the confit garlic oil and a pinch of black pepper. Blitz until you have a smooth green sauce, then taste and season with flaky salt and freshly ground black pepper to your liking.

To cook the pasta and serve

Bring a large saucepan of water to the boil over a high heat. Season well with salt, stir, then add the pasta and stir again. Cook the pasta until it is al dente, meaning that it is cooked through, but still has some bite to it (usually about 2 minutes less than the recommended cooking time listed on the packet).

Put the green sauce in the pan that contains the leeks, stir to combine and warm over a low heat. Lift the just cooked pasta out of the boiling water with tongs and put it in the pan. Sprinkle with a handful of parmesan, pour in about 80 ml (2 fl oz/⅓ cup) of the pasta water and toss everything together energetically with the tongs or a wooden spoon to emulsify. Don't stop tossing the pasta until the sauce has thickened a little and coats every piece of pasta. Serve straight away, with a block of parmesan on the table for people to grate over the dish themselves.

Cavatelli with squid and XO sauce

SERVES 4

2 large fresh squid (about 500 g/
1 lb 2 oz), cleaned by your fishmonger

60 ml (2 fl oz/¼ cup)
extra-virgin olive oil

4 garlic cloves, finely sliced

1 small shallot, finely chopped

pinch of chilli flakes

1 tomato, cut into wedges,
then halved on an angle

30 ml (1 fl oz/⅛ cup) white wine

1 tablespoon XO sauce

60 ml (2 fl oz/¼ cup) water

450 g (1 lb) Fresh cavatelli
pasta (page 169)

To make the sauce

Slice the squid into rough pieces 2–3 cm (¾–1¼ in) in size.

Heat 2 tablespoons of the olive oil in a wide frying pan over a low–medium heat and add the garlic, shallots and chilli flakes. Sauté until the garlic and shallots are golden and fragrant, then add the tomato, a pinch of flaky salt and freshly ground black pepper, and stir, leaving the tomato to cook and release its juices for about 3 minutes.

Pour in the white wine and simmer for 2 minutes to allow the alcohol to cook off. Add the XO sauce and the water, and bring the sauce to a gentle simmer for 5 minutes. At this point you want there to be a nice amount of liquid in the pan – if it looks at all dry, pour in a little more water. Pour the sauce into a vessel and set aside.

To cook the squid and pasta

Heat the remaining olive oil in the frying pan over a medium–high heat. When the oil is hot, add the squid and sear until the pieces are just cooked, about 3–4 minutes.

While the squid is cooking, bring a large saucepan of water to the boil, then season well with salt and stir. Drop the cavatelli in and cook until they float to the surface – this should take 2–3 minutes.

Reduce the heat under the squid slightly and pour the XO and tomato sauce back into the pan, along with 30 ml (1 fl oz/⅛ cup) of the pasta water. Stir to emulsify and simmer gently for 2 minutes.

To serve

When the pasta is cooked, lift the pasta out of the water using tongs or a sieve, and put it directly in the frying pan with the sauce, along with another 30–60 ml (1–2 fl oz/⅛–¼ cup) of the pasta water. Stir energetically with the tongs or a wooden spoon to emulsify. Keep the sauce at a steady simmer for 2 minutes over a medium heat – you want to see bubbles forming around the sides of the pan. If the pasta needs more sauce, add another splash of pasta water and keep tossing until you have a silky sauce and the pasta is well covered. Serve straight away.

Pappardelle with broad beans, peas and veal ragu

In Bologna I ate a memorable bowl of ragu full of young broad beans, which inspired this recipe. The sauce was surprisingly light for such a deep flavour, and I think it had something to do with the spring beans and also that the sauce's base was white rather than red. I use veal, white wine, parmesan rinds and stock to create a sort of ragu bianco that is tossed with the slightly bitter broad beans and sweeter peas. At the restaurant I add minced mortadella and prosciutto, which you can do if you are not kosher or halal. This creates a creamy, luscious ragu when tossed with a splash of pasta water and home-made egg pasta – preferably strands of pappardelle – although it is also delicious with dried pasta.

SERVES 4–5

450 g (1 lb) broad (fava) beans in their pods

2 tablespoons extra-virgin olive oil, plus extra for drizzling

500 g (1 lb 2 oz) veal shoulder, minced (ground)

20 g (¾ oz) butter

8 garlic cloves, finely chopped

150 g (5½ oz) minced mortadella (optional)

50 g (1¾ oz) minced prosciutto (optional)

125 ml (4 fl oz/½ cup) white wine

375 ml (12½ fl oz/1½ cups) Chicken stock (page 228)

2 parmesan rinds (optional)

1 teaspoon fennel seeds, crushed in a mortar and pestle

1 teaspoon chilli flakes

¼ teaspoon freshly grated nutmeg

440 g (15½ oz) fresh pappardelle (Fresh egg pasta, page 166) or a dried pasta, such as tagliatelle

120 g (4½ oz) fresh peas picked from their shells or frozen baby peas

50 g (1¾ oz) parmesan, grated on a microplane, plus extra to serve

To prepare the broad beans

Pick the beans out of their long pods. Bring a saucepan of salted water to the boil and blanch the beans for about 40 seconds, until just cooked. Strain the beans, then shock them in iced water for 1 minute. Once cool, remove them from the iced water and peel the outer skins off the beans. Discard the skins and set the beans aside in a bowl.

To make the sauce

Heat 1 tablespoon of the olive oil in a heavy-based or cast-iron frying pan over a medium heat. When the oil is hot, brown the minced veal in two batches, seasoning each batch with a quarter teaspoon of salt. Set the cooked meat aside in a bowl and return the empty frying pan to the stove.

Melt the butter and remaining oil over a low–medium heat and add the garlic, gently frying until it is golden and fragrant. If you are using the mortadella and prosciutto, add them to the pan and fry with the garlic for a few minutes, then pour in the wine and bring to a vigorous simmer for 2 minutes for the wine to cook off. Return the meat to the pan and stir to combine. Pour in the chicken stock and add the parmesan rinds, and bring the sauce to a vigorous simmer for a minute. Season with the fennel seeds, chilli flakes, nutmeg and a pinch of flaky salt and freshly ground black pepper. Reduce the heat to low, partially cover the pan with a lid and cook at a steady simmer for about 20–25 minutes. If the sauce is looking dry at any point, add a little more chicken stock 60 ml (2 fl oz/¼ cup) at a time. Taste and season further to your liking with salt and pepper.

To cook the pasta and serve

While the ragu is simmering, bring a large saucepan of water to the boil. Season well with salt and stir (the water should taste well seasoned, but you should not recoil from salt overload). Add the pasta to the saucepan and stir again. If you are using fresh pasta made with my recipe, cook for 2–3 minutes; if you are using dried pasta, cook until it is al dente, meaning that it is cooked through but still has some bite to it (this is usually about 2 minutes less than the recommended cooking time listed on the packet).

Remove the parmesan rinds from the sauce. Lift the pasta out of the water using tongs and put it in the frying pan with the ragu, along with the broad beans, peas, parmesan, 60 ml (2 fl oz/¼ cup) of the pasta water and a generous drizzle of olive oil. Toss the pasta energetically with the tongs or a wooden spoon to emulsify until you have a silky, creamy sauce. Keep the sauce at a steady simmer over a low–medium heat as you stir – you want to see bubbles forming around the sides of the pan. If the pasta needs more sauce, add another 60 ml (2 fl oz/¼ cup) of the pasta water and keep tossing until the pasta is well covered. Divide the pasta among serving plates, grate over a little more parmesan and serve straight away.

Paccheri with tuna and guanciale amatriciana

In Procida, an island off the coast of Naples in southern Italy, I booked dinner one night at a plain but beautiful restaurant with a view of the ocean. There I ate a meal with Rapha and a couple of friends that lingered in my mind as something I wanted to try making myself: an amatriciana with tuna. At first I was confused by the idea of adding tuna to this classic Roman dish, but after ordering it I found the fish paired wonderfully with the guanciale (cured pork cheek). Although there is plenty of debate around how to properly make amatriciana, the addition of tuna means this recipe is not trying to be traditional at all – although, as with any good amatriciana, it calls for good guanciale, as well as very good tinned tomatoes to go with it. I love serving this sauce with paccheri or calamarata pasta, a thick ring shape originating from Naples, but a short pasta shape, such as rigatoni, would work well too.

SERVES 2–3

400 g (14 oz) good quality <u>whole peeled tinned tomatoes</u>

120 g (4½ oz) <u>guanciale</u> (ask the butcher or deli to cut the meat into slices 1 cm/½ in thick)

3 tablespoons <u>extra-virgin olive oil</u>

60 ml (2 fl oz/¼ cup) <u>white wine</u>

½ teaspoon <u>chilli flakes</u>

220 g (8 oz) <u>paccheri pasta</u>

200 g (7 oz) fresh <u>tuna steak</u>

2 tablespoons <u>pecorino</u>, grated

1 tablespoon <u>parmesan</u>, grated

handful of <u>flat-leaf (Italian) parsley</u>, finely chopped

To make the sauce

Put the tomatoes in a bowl and crush them with your hands so that they are in small, rough pieces.

Slice the guanciale into strips 5 cm (2 in) wide, then put it in a wide frying pan over a low–medium heat, with 1 tablespoon of the olive oil. Fry the guanciale until it has rendered quite a bit of fat, turned a golden colour and is crisp at the edges, about 10–15 minutes. Try not to move the meat around too much – you want to maximise contact with the hot pan so it will get crispy. Using tongs or a slotted spoon, put the now crisp guanciale on a plate, leaving as much oil in the pan as possible. Set the guanciale aside.

Pour the white wine into the pan, leaving it to bubble and the alcohol to cook off for about 30 seconds. Add the tomatoes, the chilli flakes and a very generous pinch of flaky salt and freshly ground black pepper, and stir. Bring the sauce to a gentle simmer, then leave it to cook over a low heat for about 15 minutes, stirring occasionally. By this time the sauce should look rich and the fat should be coming to the surface. It should taste deep in flavour but if not, let it go a little longer – an extra 5–10 minutes should be enough.

Add three-quarters of the guanciale to the sauce (saving some for garnish at the end), and leave to gently simmer over a low heat.

To cook the pasta

While the sauce is simmering, bring a large saucepan of water to the boil over a high heat, then season with salt (making sure the water tastes well seasoned) and stir. Add the pasta and stir to prevent it sticking together. Cook until it is al dente (usually 2 minutes less than the recommended cooking time on the packet).

To cook the tuna and serve

While the pasta is cooking and the sauce is thickening, cook the tuna. Heat 2 tablespoons of olive oil in a frying pan over a medium–high heat. When the oil is very hot, place the tuna in the pan and sear for a minute on each side until it has just cooked through (don't overcook it). Season each side with salt and pepper and then put the cooked tuna into the sauce, increasing the heat to medium–high and breaking the tuna apart with a wooden spoon.

When the pasta is cooked, lift it out of the water and put it into the sauce. Add the cheeses, stirring continuously to make sure they melt and don't coagulate. Pour in 60 ml (2 fl oz/¼ cup) of the pasta water, a splash of olive oil and the parsley. Toss energetically with a wooden spoon or tongs to emulsify. If the sauce is looking at all dry, pour in a little more pasta water and continue to toss the pasta. Serve in bowls with the reserved crispy guanciale on top.

Tagliatelle with prawns and nduja pangrattato

I have decided that the prawn heads do the heaviest-lifting in this recipe. There is so much secret flavour lying in those little heads. By crushing them with a wooden spoon in a hot pan you release their sweet juices, giving this pasta sauce a deep, savoury flavour. It is at this point that I steal a crispy prawn head from the pan and suck out the juices, salty and sweet at the same time, chef's snack. Covering the heads with water and reducing to create a prawn head stock changes the nature of this pasta from a simple prawn pasta to a rich, fragrant seafood sauce. On top of prawn pasta I like crispy fried nduja breadcrumbs for texture and a layer of spice, also known as pangrattato. Using leftover focaccia for the breadcrumbs is my preference.

SERVES 4

PRAWN HEAD STOCK

60 ml (2 fl oz/¼ cup) extra-virgin olive oil

1 garlic bulb, sliced in half horizontally

3 onions, roughly chopped

1 fennel bulb, roughly chopped

5 bay leaves

20 uncooked prawn heads and shells

125 ml (4 fl oz/½ cup) white wine

3 tablespoons tomato paste

1 teaspoon salt

875 ml (29½ fl oz/3½ cups) water

To clean the prawns

Gently twist the prawn's head to remove it. Put the head in a bowl and set aside. Then, on the underside of the prawn, dig your thumb under the edge of the shell where the head was attached and peel the shell off. Next, remove the tail with a gentle pull. Put the shell and tail in the bowl with the prawn head. Now devein the prawn by running a sharp knife along its back (try not to slice too deep), then with the tip of the knife carefully pull out the black intestinal tract and discard. Repeat this process with the rest of the prawns, and give them a good rinse, then slice each prawn into three or four pieces and put in the fridge until ready to use.

To make the prawn head stock

Heat the olive oil in a large, heavy-based saucepan with a lid over a low heat, and add the garlic, vegetables and bay leaves. Stir and cook until the vegetables have softened and become translucent and fragrant, about 10–15 minutes.

Increase the heat slightly to medium–high, then add the prawn heads and shells and cook for 5 minutes, pressing down on the heads to release their juices into the pan. Pour in the wine, let it bubble up and simmer for 2 minutes to cook off the alcohol.

Reduce the heat to low–medium and add the tomato paste. Stir and leave to simmer gently for 3 minutes, or until the tomato has deepened in colour and thickened. Season with the salt and a generous pinch of freshly ground black pepper.

SAUCE

20 raw prawns, shells
and heads left on

250 g (9 oz) cherry tomatoes

60 ml (2 fl oz) extra-virgin olive oil

10 garlic cloves, finely sliced

1 red chilli, finely sliced

125 ml (4 fl oz/½ cup) white wine

500 ml (17 fl oz/2 cups)
prawn head stock

440 g (15½ oz) fresh tagliatelle
(Fresh egg pasta, page 168)
or use dry tagliatelle

handful of flat-leaf (Italian)
parsley, finely chopped

15 g (½ oz) unsalted butter

100 g (3½ oz) Nduja pangrattato
(page 223) to serve

Cover the prawn heads and vegetables with the water, increase the heat slightly and bring to the boil for 2 minutes, then reduce the heat to low–medium and leave the stock to simmer gently with the lid partially on for about 30 minutes to an hour. Every so often check on the stock, give it a stir and press down on the heads again until the stock tastes rich and delicious.

When you're happy with the flavour, strain the stock and discard the vegetables, shells and heads, setting the stock aside until you are ready to use it.

To make the sauce

Bring a large saucepan of water to the boil over a high heat. Once boiling, season well with salt and stir (the water should taste well seasoned, but you should not recoil from salt overload). Slice an 'x' into the bottom of each of the cherry tomatoes with a sharp paring knife, then blanch them for about 20 seconds until the skins lift up. Use a slotted spoon to lift the tomatoes onto a large plate to cool. Keep the water in the saucepan topped up and at a boil as you will cook the pasta in it soon. When the tomatoes are cool enough, peel the skins and any stems off the tomatoes and discard them. Set the tomato flesh aside.

Heat 3 tablespoons of the olive oil in a wide, heavy-based frying pan over a low heat, and add the garlic and chilli. Cook for 1–2 minutes until the garlic smells fragrant and is just starting to turn golden, but don't take it any further otherwise you risk it burning.

Add the peeled tomatoes and mash them gently with the back of a wooden spoon so they break down into the garlicky chilli oil.

Increase the heat to medium–high, pour in the wine and cook off the alcohol until the liquid has reduced by half, about 2 minutes.

Pour in 500 ml (17 fl oz/2 cups) of the prawn head stock, stir and keep the sauce at a steady simmer over a medium heat for about 10 minutes or until the sauce has reduced by half. Spoon the sauce out of the pan and wipe the pan clean.

To cook the pasta and serve

Put the pasta into the pot of boiling salted water that you used for blanching the tomatoes and stir. Cook until it is al dente, meaning that it is cooked through but still has some bite to it (this is usually about 2 minutes less than the recommended cooking time listed on the packet).

When the pasta is 2 minutes away from being ready, heat the remaining tablespoon of olive oil in the clean frying pan over a medium–high heat. When the pan is hot, add the chopped prawn meat and sauté until they are just cooked, about 2 minutes (don't overcook them at this stage, as the prawns will continue cooking in the heat of the pasta and sauce). Pour the sauce back into the pan, give it a shake and let the flavours come together.

Using tongs, lift the pasta out of the water and put it into the pan, along with 30 ml (1 fl oz/⅛ cup) of pasta water, the parsley, a glug of olive oil and the butter. Stir and toss the pasta energetically with tongs or a wooden spoon to emulsify until you have a silky sauce. Keep the sauce at a steady simmer over a low–medium heat as you stir – you want to see bubbles around the sides of the pan. Divide the pasta between plates and top with the nduja pangrattato.

Sweets

Watermelon and cherries on ice 202
Fresh mint tea 202
Raiff 205
Rugelach 206
Pistachio and almond amaretti biscuits 210
Vermouth poached cherries and mascarpone 213
On eating clementinot (mandarins) with my dad 214

Our lunchtime feast at my great aunty's apartment was coming to an end. The big lace tablecloth that dressed the dining table was now covered in matbukha and oil stains. Plates of finished food had been swiftly lifted off the table to take their new place beside the kitchen sink. Most of the family were reclining in their seats, full and happy after eating mounds of couscous, vegetables cooked in cinnamon and onion-laden meatballs. My sister and I started flicking through old family photo albums, and pointed out the beautiful-looking Moroccan wedding biscuits that appeared in the background of a photo. Next minute, my great aunty handed us a box of the same kind of celebration biscuits, which she had made and kept frozen for a future occasion. They were even more beautiful than those in the picture.

Dessert isn't fancy at my great aunty's place. She poured tea and served generous slices cut from a whole watermelon, along with a bunch of summer grapes. A slightly questionable cake that someone bought from a nearby supermarket was pulled out of its plastic package too.

I turned around to listen to what my great aunty and her cousin were whispering about. From the broken mix of Hebrew and Arabic I garnered that they had spent time that morning making a batch of raiff. The cousin wanted to put them out for everyone, but my great aunty wanted to save them – something about them being time consuming to make and too special. I found this scene humorous and so classic: two old Jewish women making sure that the family didn't devour all of their handiwork too quickly. Their back and forth turned to agreement as they decided that they at least wanted my dad to taste the biscuits made from the same recipe that his late mother used when he was growing up.

I was lucky enough to have a bite and for a moment I was taken back to my own childhood, eating the same biscuits baked by my father's parents. It is the simplest of biscuits, full of golden sesame seeds and aniseedy fennel seeds. Each biscuit typically has a ruffled imprint down the centre, created by gently pinching the dough. It seemed only right that I learn how to make them, so I convinced great aunt Melani and

and her younger cousin Mimi to give me the recipe for this treasure. As they blurted out the recipe my aunty Marcel hastily wrote it down in Hebrew in my journal for me to decode later.

Although my dad grew up surrounded by beautiful food traditions and a family full of excellent cooks, he spent most of his teenage years and young adult life looking after his newly arrived parents. His mother had been in a traumatic car accident that left her quadriplegic for the rest of her life. Until their passing, both of my grandparents weren't able to work full-time and they spoke only a little English. Their native language was a mix of Judeo-Moroccan Arabic and Hebrew; before immigrating to Australia they had only just learnt to speak Hebrew fluently. My dad worked hard to look after both of his parents and as such didn't have a heap of spare time to cook, but he would always watch as the food was prepared – and of course eat it.

On a warm afternoon before the Jewish holiday of Rosh Hashanah began one year, I baked raiff biscuits with my dad. As I read the recipe that my aunty had written in my journal for me, I realised that she hadn't included a method, only some rough quantities written messily in Hebrew. My dad deciphered the text and we started mixing the ingredients together. I was taken by my dad's natural ease in making the raiff. Although we had no written directions, he knew exactly the consistency the dough was meant to be and naturally created the ruffled seams down the centre of the biscuits from his memories of watching his mother do it.

Seeing my dad's fingers roll out the dough and indent the unbaked biscuits is a food memory now etched into my mind. That he baked biscuits he had never made before, but knew how to make from years of watching his mother do the same, reaffirms my belief that some of the best food is created in homes and that food traditions can often be passed down from generation to generation without you even noticing, until the day comes that you too make the dish.

Later in the evening, towards the end of our Rosh Hashanah meal, my dad cheekily gestured that I should secretly put away a box of the biscuits – just like my aunties did a few months earlier – so that we could eat them with our coffee the next morning.

My general approach to dessert mirrors my great aunt's in its simplicity. I often plate some freshly baked raiff and serve them with tay im naana (Fresh mint tea, page 202) and whichever fruit is in season. If it is summer, then sliced Watermelon and cherries on ice (page 202) is a beautiful idea; if it is winter, a bowl full of mandarins for people to peel while sipping on tea is a nice way to end the meal. The Pistachio and almond amaretti biscuits (page 210) in this chapter are a satisfyingly simple sweet to make and enjoy as dessert with tea or a coffee. I began making amaretti biscuits as they reminded me of the Moroccan almond cookies that my late Saba Rafael used to make for Passover. Whenever I bake them I have to double the amount so I can drop a batch at Rapha's grandparents' place. Papa Bernie loves the chewy pistachio and almond biscuits so much that he hides them in his pantry and pulls them out only for special guests and for himself with a morning espresso. One of my favourite ways to finish a meal at my house is with a dessert that I used to serve at the restaurant: a plate of amaretti biscuits alongside whipped mascarpone and cherries poached in vermouth (page 213). I also love all stone fruits and would just as easily serve the amaretti with poached peaches or plums and fresh mint tea.

Watermelon and cherries on ice

Fresh mint tea

After a gluttonous meal I don't feel like eating much more than a plate of chilled fruit for dessert. When they are in season, red berries, stone fruit such as nectarines and peaches, cherries, a juicy watermelon and ripe figs are a dreamy way to end a feast. If I am in the mood to bake, I also love a simple fruit-filled crostata or a frangipane tart with a confident drop of chantilly cream. Usually, though, I find watermelon and cherries piled on ice the most satisfying.

My dad is good at choosing the perfect watermelon. He knocks on them, turns them upside down and around, and then he takes the selected watermelon home and slices it up very delicately. He is careful about the process, uses a sharp knife and is rewarded with perfect pieces of sweet, crisp watermelon.

Choose a watermelon that feels heavy – this will indicate a high water content – and that resonates like a drum when you tap it – if it sounds hollow, this can mean that the flesh inside has cracks in it. A yellow patch on one side of the watermelon will show that it was ripe when it was picked. Once you have your watermelon home, slice it on a clean and garlic-free chopping board, and make sure it is very cold when you serve it. On a hot day, I like to bring the watermelon to the table on a pile of ice, the cherries strewn over the top.

Mint tea, or tay im naana, plays a key role in my Moroccan family's hospitality; it is served to guests whatever the occasion. My dad makes it with fresh mint leaves and a little sugar to sweeten. It's as simple to make as putting a bunch of fresh mint leaves and a small amount of sugar in your most beautiful teapot and filling it to the top with boiling water. Let the mint steep for 15 minutes, then pour into individual glasses and serve with biscuits and fresh fruit.

Raiff

Raiff are simple Moroccan tea biscuits made with sesame and fennel seeds. Although sesame and fennel may seem an odd combination for a biscuit, they pair well together – especially when the raiff are accompanied by a pot of fresh, sweet mint tea. I love creating the ruffled imprint down the centre by gently pinching the dough. My dad and I make raiff together. The dough comes together quickly and each biscuit looks slightly different depending on who is slicing and pinching the mixture. These biscuits are a familiar, nostalgic bite for me. Serve them with fresh fruit, hot tea and maybe a plate of dates too.

<u>MAKES ABOUT 65 BISCUITS</u>

250 ml (8½ fl oz/1 cup) <u>extra-virgin olive oil</u>

250 ml (8½ fl oz/1 cup) <u>water</u>

6 tablespoons <u>sesame seeds</u>

2 tablespoons <u>fennel seeds</u>

1 teaspoon <u>salt</u>

115 g (4 oz/½ cup) <u>caster sugar</u> (superfine)

3 teaspoons <u>baking powder</u>

3 teaspoons <u>vanilla extract</u>

600 g (1 lb 5 oz) <u>plain (all-purpose) flour</u>, plus you may need an extra 50 g (1¾ oz)

Preheat the oven to 200°C (390°F).

To make the dough

Put everything besides the flour in a large bowl and stir together. The water and oil will remain separate, but will come together when you add the flour.

Add the flour a cup at a time, constantly bringing the ingredients together with your hands or a wooden spoon, until you have added all of the flour. The mixture should feel soft and slightly wet, but not sticky, so add a little more flour if it needs it until you reach that consistency.

To roll the biscuits

When the dough has come together, roll it into a log about 50 cm (19¾ in) long on a lightly floured surface. Slice the log into six pieces, then using either a rolling pin or the palms of your hands, roll each piece of dough into a rectangle about 2.5–3 mm (⅛ in) thick.

Slice each rectangle into pieces about 3 cm (1¼ in) wide. Then, beginning at the top of the biscuit, use your thumb and index finger to pinch a sort of seam down the centre to create a ruffled pattern. Repeat for all of the biscuits, then place them on baking trays lined with baking paper.

To bake and serve

Bake for about 15 minutes until golden – keep an eye on them to make sure they don't burn. Leave them to cool completely on a rack. They may be a little soft when you first take them out of the oven, but they will crisp up as they cool down.

Note: The raiff will keep in an airtight container for a couple of weeks.

Rugelach

When I was learning to make rugelach with my safta, she made the point that her recipe is over forty years old. Of all the sweets that she makes, these pastries are my favourite crisp and flaky and filled with chocolate or jam. The recipe is a special one, carrying many memories for the Ashkenazi Jewish diaspora. When I watch my safta make them, I am mesmerised by the way her fingers move as she rolls the dough into little crescents.

She puts these sweets together so naturally, and I try to picture all the previous times she has made them, when my mum was a child and her family was new to Australia.

As I attempted to weigh the ingredients so that I could create a functional recipe, my safta, eyebrows raised, questioned me: 'Oh, you want to weigh it all? Really?' She has never understood the need for measurements. I appreciate her style of cooking, all intuition and the memory of women and family cooking together over time. This is a recipe written in her heart, but never on paper. I think I am the first to record her process for making rugelach. Perhaps I too follow my safta's lead, more often than not keeping recipes in my heart, struggling to specify quantities and instead

making it the next time by feel – maybe a reason why this journey of collecting recipes, with the need to note them down with rigid measurements, has been a complicated but very important one for me.

This recipe includes the ingredients for two fillings: one a chocolate and nut filling, and the other a jam filling. My safta usually uses half the dough to make the jam filling and the other half to make the chocolate filling, which you can do too. Depending on her mood safta will either roll the dough into croissant-like shapes or into a log that is sliced into swirled discs. I have included the method for both ways.

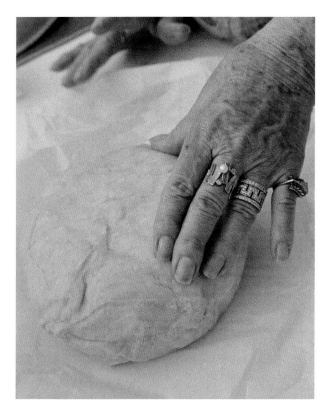

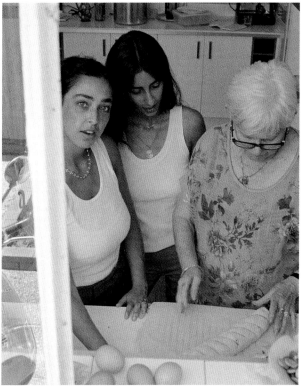

Rugelach

225 g (8 oz/1½ cups)
self-raising flour

225 g (8 oz/1½ cups) plain
(all-purpose) flour

3 tablespoons caster sugar (superfine)

pinch of salt

250 g (9 oz) unsalted butter,
chilled and diced plus extra,
melted, for brushing

3 eggs, separated

300 ml (10 fl oz) thickened
(whipping) cream

1 vanilla bean

CHOCOLATE FILLING

200 g (7 oz) 54.5% dark Belgian
chocolate (I use Callebaut brand),
blitzed into a fine consistency

200 g (7 oz) walnuts, roughly
crushed into a coarse texture

1–2 tablespoons drinking chocolate

½ tablespoon ground cinnamon

raw sugar for sprinkling

JAM FILLING

50 g (1¾ oz) walnuts, roughly
chopped into a coarse texture

40 g (1½ oz) 54.5% dark
Belgian chocolate, blitzed
into a fine consistency

1 tablespoon drinking chocolate

200 g (7 oz) good quality
raspberry jam

raw sugar for sprinkling

To make the dough

Stir the flours, sugar and salt in a bowl with your hands. Add the butter and rub it into the flour with your fingers until the mixture resembles coarse breadcrumbs.

Add the yolks to the flour mixture, along with the thickened cream. Split the vanilla bean and scrape in the seeds. Very briefly and gently mix until the dough has just come together. Be careful not to overmix the dough.

Wrap the dough tightly in baking paper and then, like my safta, put it in an old plastic bag in the fridge to rest overnight.

Cut the dough into two pieces. Lightly flour a clean surface, then roll out each of the pieces with a rolling pin into a flat disc about 1 cm (½ in) thick.

To make chocolate-filled rugelach

Preheat the oven to 200°C (390°F). Line two baking trays with baking paper and brush the paper with melted butter.

Mix the chocolate, walnuts, drinking chocolate and cinnamon together.

Paint one of the flattened discs with melted butter and sprinkle over enough of the chocolate and nut mix to cover the disc, then drizzle a bit of melted butter and sprinkle some raw sugar over the top. Slice the disc into eight or twelve triangles in the same way that you would cut a pizza. Next roll each wedge up, starting at the wide edge and pinching the pointed end into the dough.

Put the rolled rugelach onto the baking trays, leaving at least two fingers of space between each. Paint the tops with more melted butter and sprinkle with raw sugar.

Bake for 30 minutes until golden, then cool on a rack.

To make jam-filled rugelach

Preheat the oven to 200°C (390°F). Line a baking tray with baking paper and brush the paper with melted butter.

Combine the walnuts, dark chocolate and drinking chocolate in a bowl.

Spread the second flattened disc with jam, then sprinkle over the chocolate nut filling. Roll the disc into a long log, pressing the edges of the pastry together at both ends. Next cut a series of incisions 2 cm (¾ in) wide into the dough widthways along the length of the log, but don't slice all the way through to the tray or the jam will spill out during baking. Brush the top of the log with melted butter and sprinkle with raw sugar.

Bake for about 30 minutes, then cool on a rack. Once cool, slice the log all the way through to create individual pieces of rugelach.

Pistachio and almond amaretti biscuits

These amaretti are ideal dessert eating or very good in the morning with a coffee. It's important for the biscuit's texture to be somewhere between chewy and crunchy, so make sure you whip the egg whites until they are almost like meringue before combining them with the nut and sugar mixture.

MAKES 30 BISCUITS

3 egg whites (total weight about 80 g / 2¾ oz)

400 g (14 oz) caster sugar (superfine)

250 g (9 oz) unsalted pistachio nuts

230 g (8 oz) ground almonds

1 vanilla bean, split lengthways and seeds scraped

COATING

100 g (3½ oz) caster sugar (superfine)

100 g (3½ oz) icing (confectioners') sugar

Preheat the oven to 190°C (375°F) and line two baking trays with baking paper.

To make the dough

In an electric mixer or using electric beaters, whip the egg whites until fluffy, then slowly add half of the caster sugar 1 tablespoon at a time until stiff peaks have formed.

Pulse the pistachios in a food processor until they are the texture of fine breadcrumbs, but slightly coarser than the ground almonds.

Mix the pistachios, ground almonds, the rest of the caster sugar and the vanilla bean seeds in a large bowl. Add half of the beaten egg whites in the mixture and, using your hands, bring the mixture together to form a soft, sticky dough. Add the rest of the egg white mixture and combine with your hands.

To roll and coat the biscuits

Scoop out a lump of dough weighing about 30 g (1 oz), then gently roll it between your hands into a walnut-sized ball. Dust the ball lightly in the caster sugar, then dust more heavily in the icing sugar and put it on the baking tray. Repeat until you have used up all of the dough.

To bake and serve

Bake for about 15–18 minutes. The bottom of the biscuits should be golden brown and the top cracked. Leave them to cool completely on a wire rack. They may be soft in the middle when you first take them out of the oven, but will soon crisp up as they cool down.

Note: The amaretti will keep in an airtight container for a couple of weeks. Eat them with a coffee or serve with the Vermouth poached cherries and mascarpone (page 213) for a decadent dessert.

Note: The texture of the amaretti may vary each time you make them, but don't be alarmed. It will be affected by the oil content of the nuts, moisture content of the egg whites and temperature of your kitchen, all of which can differ from batch to batch.

Vermouth poached cherries and mascarpone

Fresh cherries are cooked in sweet vermouth, water, sugar and vanilla bean until they are tender and soft (but not shrivelled!), then lemon juice is stirred through to provide a hit of acidity. Plating the just cooked fruit with creamy mascarpone and the syrup from the poaching liquid makes for a festive sight. Serve this dish with a bunch of spoons around the rim for people to messily dig in at the same time, and accompany it with some good quality, fragrant vermouth on ice – I love Saison vermouth, if you can get your hands on a bottle.

SERVES 3

POACHED CHERRIES

400 g (14 oz) cherries, plus an extra 100 g (3½ oz) to serve

125 ml (4 fl oz/½ cup) sweet vermouth

60 ml (2 fl oz/¼ cup) water

50 g (1¾ oz) caster sugar (superfine)

1 vanilla bean

1 tablespoon lemon juice

MASCARPONE

60 ml (2 fl oz/¼ cup) thick cream (double/heavy), chilled

45 g (1½ oz) caster sugar (superfine)

250 g (9 oz) mascarpone

To make the mascarpone

In an electric mixer or using electric beaters, beat the cream and sugar together on high speed until soft peaks form. Gently fold the mascarpone into the cream, then chill in the fridge until needed.

To poach the cherries and make the syrup

Pull the stems off 400 g (14 oz) of the cherries and discard the stems. Put the cherries in a saucepan together with the vermouth, water, sugar and vanilla bean over a low–medium heat. Gently simmer until the cherries are just tender, about 10 minutes – be careful not to cook them too long, as you don't want them soft and shrivelled. Turn off the heat, pour in the lemon juice and stir. Cover the cherries for 5 minutes, then take them out of the liquid and set aside. Gently simmer the liquid over a low heat until it thickens a little and becomes syrupy so that it coats the back of a spoon.

To serve

When the syrup has cooled, put the poached cherries on a serving plate, spoon the syrup over them, then dollop the mascarpone beside the cherries. Scatter the fresh cherries on top and serve.

On eating clementinot (mandarins) with my dad

I was happy wandering among the new season vegetables at the small market, but I was most excited when I saw the mandarin stand, stacked with baskets of the bright orange fruit. I started thinking of ways to put them on my menu: maybe a tall sponge with layers of chantilly cream spiked with mandarin syrup and the skin of the fruit candied on top ... or mandarin granita? They are my dad's favourite fruit and I decided to buy him a few. I grabbed a basketfull and went home happily. I invited my dad over, and we ate a couple of them over the sink later that afternoon.

Clementinot. I asked my dad to tell me about his love of this citrus, and what followed was a wholehearted conversation about his devotion to this plump fruit. His descriptions of this mandarin were almost otherwordly, full of ahhhs and sweet sighs. My dad's favourite time to eat a clementine is at night-time, just before bed. He stands over the kitchen sink, peeling back the layer of skin. He often eats them so quickly that he bites his tongue or chokes on the sweet juices, the sink collecting any citrus spritz lost in the process.

I was curious as to how he knows which mandarins to pick. His answer was simple, 'I go to the supermarket and I try all of them.' This genuine need to feel and taste each fruit before making a decision made me laugh and reminded me of myself. 'Yes, I try all of them there, I don't want to get stuck with the wrong mandarin.' He wants the sweetest one he can get his hands on, no matter the cost. My dad's advice continues, 'You should take the mandarin, peel it to expose the flesh, and each segment should be firm on the outside, but when you bite into it the juice should explode into your mouth.' He is adamant that you do not want the mandarin to be soft. 'And they should be seedless. The pips are disturbing you from eating them quickly because you have to deal with them, you have to pick them out.'

We were quickly wrapped up in a layer of nostalgia. My dad was transported to moments he shared with his own father before he recently passed. Every day after work my dad went to sit with my saba. They would watch TV, eat clementines and artichokes together, and doze off on the couch. You could hear the emotion in my dad's voice. 'Every time. Every time I went to sit there with him, he would get up, hardly able to walk to the kitchen, he was so unwell, and come back with a plate of anavim (grapes), clementinot or artichokes and say "come on, eat".' And then I realise that my dad does the same thing. There are many ways he goes about sharing his warmth and generosity, ways I want to follow, but one of the most important is sharing a piece of fruit with me and my sisters, his daughters. When I hear that familiar sound coming from the kitchen sink, my dad chewing through citrus flesh and juice, I will call out to him. Instead of it irritating him, he just wants to share, to peel the clementine for me and give me the whole fruit if I want it. I never take the whole thing, usually a few segments at the most, and then I leave my dad to enjoy the rest before he closes the blinds and goes to sleep for the night.

Fridge and Pantry

Garlic and chilli oil 223
Pangrattato 223
Home-made labneh 224
Vegetable stock 227
Chicken stock 228
Pickled radishes and turnips 229

Fridge and pantry; the heartbeat of the kitchen. Behind these doors is the foundation of your dish. You probably already have a store of quiet, unassuming ingredients lying in your fridge and pantry that you can use to build flavour and texture. Start with finding a good quality bottle of extra-virgin olive oil that you can use for most dishes. Always have a couple of tangy wine vinegars in the pantry to add when you want to brighten a dish. I also have some other essential, sometimes slightly unexpected fridge and pantry items, mostly savoury things, that I always keep around to create fragrant, flavourful bases – specifically good anchovies (to melt into and strengthen the base of just about any sauce), fish sauce, yuzu ponzu, dijon mustard, white cooking wine, good quality sweet butter, kombu and baby capers.

There is extra flavour everywhere. Don't wash away the browned bits stuck to the bottom of a pan: rather, splash a bit of wine or stock into the pan, scrape the bits up, whisk in some butter and you have created a sauce to go with whatever it is you just seared. Don't waste flavour. Keep the rind from a block of parmesan and put it in a ragu or soup that you are simmering on the stove – the addition of simple elements like this will add richness and flavour to your cooking.

Here are the things I reach for in my fridge and pantry that are my essentials for building flavour and texture in a whole range of dishes:

OILS AND FATS
→ Good quality extra-virgin olive oil
→ Good quality sweet butter
→ Schmaltz: one of my favourite fats to use to layer in richness; Fried chicken skin, a byproduct of making your own schmaltz, is delicious as a chef's snack too or to add texture to a dish, for example crumbled over chicken livers on toast (page 42).
→ Garlic confit and its oil (pages 68, 180): having a jar of your own confit garlic in the fridge is a nice thing to have on hand to layer in a mellow, almost sweet garlic flavour to a range of dishes.

SAUCES, VINEGARS, WINE AND STOCKS
→ Colatura di alici (an anchovy oil with a similar flavour profile to fish sauce)
→ Soy sauce
→ Fish sauce
→ Chilli oil with lots of MSG
→ A collection of vinegars is important in my kitchen; I like tarragon, chardonnay and sherry vinegars. I'm slowly building up a wide range as a way to add different tangy profiles to dishes.
→ White wine for cooking
→ Chicken stock powder (don't turn your nose up at this one, it features in a lot of Jewish and other ethnic cooking)
→ Home-made chicken stock (page 228)
→ Home-made vegetable stock (page 227)

THINGS THAT ADD RICHNESS TO THE FLAVOUR BASE OF SAUCES, SOUPS AND STOCKS
→ A tin of good anchovies in olive oil: if you're using these as the base of a recipe, they don't need to be the best quality as they melt into the dish anyway, but make sure you buy anchovies packed in olive oil. When you want to serve anchovies straight from the tin – for example, with focaccia or next to radishes and butter – it is worth seeking out a higher quality tin, like Yurrita.
→ Dried shiitake
→ Kombu
→ Parmesan rinds
→ Miso paste (a good substitute for anchovies in vegetarian dishes)
→ Nduja

SALTY THINGS FOR POPS OF SAVOURINESS
→ Tins of sardines/mackerel/ sustainable fish
→ A variety of olives
→ Baby capers, both in brine and in salt
→ Bottarga (dried mullet or tuna roe)

FROZEN VEGETABLES AND DRIED LEGUMES

→ Frozen baby peas are always a good idea to have on hand.

→ Borlotti beans: sometimes you will find bags of frozen borlotti beans at Mediterranean delis; buy a bag if you come across them, as they are a good addition to soups, salads etc. when the beans are unavailable as a fresh product.

→ Artichoke bottoms for my recipe on page 155. Use frozen artichoke bottoms as the base for stuffing minced meat, not for a snack plate. You can usually find frozen artichoke bottoms at Middle Eastern and Mediterranean delis.

→ Dried chickpeas and baby beluga lentils

THINGS TO MAKE AND KEEP IN THE FRIDGE FOR EXTRA SPICE, CRUNCH OR CREAMINESS

→ Garlic and chilli oil (page 223)

→ Home-made labneh (page 224)

→ Zhoug (page 111)

→ Salsa verde (page 141)

→ Pangrattato (page 223)

→ Pickled radishes and turnips (page 229)

→ Whipped butters (page 66)

SPICES

→ Bahārāt

→ Hawayj

→ Turmeric

→ Fennel seeds

→ Smoked paprika

→ Cumin

Garlic and chilli oil

2 tablespoons extra-virgin olive oil, plus more to cover

2 garlic bulbs, cloves finely sliced

2 red chillies, finely sliced (or more, depending on how spicy you like things)

Heat the 2 tablespoons of the olive oil in a small saucepan over a low–medium heat and add the garlic and chilli, then sauté for about a minute until the garlic is a golden colour and smells fragrant. Try to get some caramelisation on the garlic too, but take care not to burn it as otherwise it will have a bitter taste. Season with salt, then pour over enough olive oil to cover the garlic and chilli, and reduce to the lowest heat. You want small bubbles to build up around the garlic and chilli, but not for the bubbles to become too intense and violent. Cook gently for about 10–15 minutes so the garlic and chilli infuse into the oil. When the garlic is soft and golden, turn the heat off. Leave to cool, then pour into a jar or container and store in the fridge for up to a week. Use as the base oil for frying in whichever dish you want.

Pangrattato

400 g (14 oz) stale or day-old focaccia (or plain bread if you don't have leftover focaccia)

2 tablespoons extra-virgin olive oil

2 garlic cloves, smashed with the back of a knife

NDUJA PANGRATTATO

40 g (1½ oz) nduja

grated zest of 1 lemon

Preheat the oven to 170°C (340°F).

Tear the focaccia into pieces and put it in a food processor. Blitz the bread until it is the consistency of fine breadcrumbs but still with some texture to it, then transfer to a wide baking tray. Pour over the olive oil, add the garlic, season with flaky salt and toss to combine. If making the nduja pangrattato, crumble in the nduja at this point and toss to combine. Spread the breadcrumb mixture across the tray in an even layer.

Toast the breadcrumb mixture for about 20–45 minutes, checking from time to time to make sure they are crisping up and not burning. The pangrattato is ready when the crumbs are golden and crisp.

Take the tray out of the oven and leave the crumbs to cool completely. If making the nduja pangrattato, add the lemon zest and toss to combine. The pangrattato will stay crisp in a sealed container in the fridge for up to a week.

Home-made labneh

MAKES 1 SMALL JAR

1 litre (34 fl oz/4 cups)
<u>full-cream (whole) milk</u>

3–4 tablespoons <u>plain yoghurt</u>

¾ teaspoon <u>salt</u>

Warm the milk in a large, heavy-based or cast-iron saucepan over a medium heat until it reaches a boil (about 90°C/195°F if you are using a thermometer), then gently simmer for 2 minutes, stirring it every now and then to prevent a skin from forming.

Take the saucepan off the heat and put it in an ice bath to cool down to 35–40°C (95–105°F) but no lower or higher.

Spoon the yoghurt into a bowl and whisk in 250 ml (8½ fl oz/1 cup) of the warm milk very thoroughly. Don't add the milk when it is too hot or you will kill the bacteria (it's the same principle as when you add warm water to yeast when making focaccia). Pour the yoghurt-milk mixture into the remaining warm milk and whisk again thoroughly to combine – this will ensure a smooth yoghurt.

Pour the yoghurt mixture into sterilised jars and seal the lids. Leave the yoghurt mixture in a warm spot, around 25°C (77°F), to set for 10 or so hours, by which time it should have thickened into yoghurt, then transfer to the fridge to chill and thicken further for at least 2 hours. (If you don't want to make labneh, the yoghurt will keep for a week in the fridge.)

Next mix the salt into the chilled yoghurt. Pour the yoghurt into a muslin (cheesecloth), tie the ends of the cloth together and hang it over a bowl in the fridge to drain for 24–48 hours, depending on how soft and creamy you want it. Draining the yoghurt for longer will give you a thicker, creamier labneh. Check it every 12 hours and when the labneh has reached your desired consistency, transfer it to an airtight container and store in the fridge for up to a week.

You can serve the labneh simply, with a bit of flaky salt and olive oil sprinkled over the top, as well as fresh herbs, such as mint or parsley, or with Crisp vegetables with lemon dressing and labneh (page 29), Fish cakes with green herbs and labneh (page 84), or pickled radishes (page 229) and charred spring onion.

If you don't have time to make labneh from scratch you can make this simple version. Take 1 litre of good quality, plain natural yoghurt, mix it in a bowl with the juice of 4 lemons, and season with about 1 tablespoon of flaky salt. Pour the yoghurt into a muslin (cheesecloth), tie the ends together and place it inside a sieve. Place the sieve over a bowl in the fridge to drain overnight until the bowl is full of liquid and you have a cheesecloth full of thick labneh.

Vegetable stock

The ingredients in this recipe and their amounts are intentionally a little vague as this stock is something you can make with almost any vegetable and whatever alliums you have in the fridge – spring onions (scallions), mushrooms, red onions – almost nothing is off limits. Leaving the skins on the vegetables means extra flavour and less work for you, and browning them in the oven first deepens the flavour of the stock. Parmesan rinds, fresh herbs, kombu and dried mushrooms give a richer, more savoury flavour, so if you have any of these in your pantry or fridge, throw them in. Make a big pot of the stock, and then keep it in the fridge to use throughout the week, or freeze it in smaller quantities to defrost and use when you need it.

MAKES ABOUT 4 LITRES

1 leek, roughly chopped

2 onions, roughly chopped

2 red onions, roughly chopped

2 carrots, roughly chopped

4 celery stalks, roughly chopped, leaves left on

1 fennel bulb, roughly chopped, fronds left on

couple of red chillies, sliced in half lengthways

handful of fresh or dried mushrooms

handful of bay leaves

bunch of any fresh herbs you have on hand, such as flat-leaf (Italian) parsley or thyme

3 tablespoons extra-virgin olive oil

pinch of paprika

Preheat the oven to 220°C (430°F).

Put all the fresh vegetables and herbs except for the celery leaves and fennel fronds on a couple of roasting trays, douse in the olive oil and season with salt, freshly ground black pepper and the paprika. Roast until golden and caramelised, about 30 minutes.

Take the vegetables out of the oven and put them in a large stockpot, add the celery leaves and fennel fronds (if you have kombu or parmesan rinds, place them in the pot too), cover completely with cold water (about 5 litres/170 fl oz) and bring to the boil over a medium heat. Reduce to a simmer and cook gently for about 1–2 hours until the stock has reduced a little and tastes savoury and full of flavour. Skim off any foam on the top of the broth, and taste and season with more salt and pepper along the way if needed.

Strain the broth, discarding the cooked vegetables, and store in the fridge for up to 5 days or in the freezer for about 6 months.

Chicken stock

One New Year's Eve we were invited to a long lunch in the garden of our friends Pete and Sunni out in Eltham. Pete cooked six chickens over a rotating charcoal spit, which we ate with flatbreads, tzatziki made by Rapha and summer tomatoes. When everyone had finished eating, Pete threw the leftover chicken bones and carcasses into a pot on the stove with a few aromatic vegetables and water. Over the course of the night anyone who walked into the kitchen topped up the water in the pot. As people relaxed in the warm evening, a chicken stock was cooking away – I found this quite beautiful. I love the idea of taking the bones of a cooked chicken and creating an overnight stock. The house smells lovely and the leftover bones are given another use. When you make the recipe below, don't season the stock too heavily – because it will be used as a base for future dishes, it should be mellow in seasoning for maximum flexibility.

MAKES ABOUT 4 LITRES

3 kg (6 lb 10 oz) mix of <u>raw chicken carcasses</u>, <u>chicken necks</u>, <u>marrow bones</u>

100 g (3½ oz) <u>butter</u> (optional; to keep this recipe kosher, substitute 170 ml/5½ fl oz/⅔ cup <u>extra-virgin olive oil</u>)

30 ml (1 fl oz) <u>extra-virgin olive oil</u>

3 <u>onions</u>, finely diced (set aside the onion skins)

½ bunch <u>celery</u>, finely diced

3 <u>carrots</u>, finely diced

1 <u>garlic bulb</u>, sliced in half horizontally

2 tablespoons <u>peppercorns</u>

6 <u>bay leaves</u>

Rinse the chicken carcasses under cold water to clean them.

Melt the butter and oil in a large stockpot over a medium heat, then add the onions, celery and carrots. Slowly sweat the vegetables until translucent, about 15 minutes, then add the garlic, peppercorns and bay leaves, plus any other leftover herbs and vegetable scraps you would like and sauté for 5 minutes. Season with a small amount of flaky salt.

Add the chicken carcasses (be mindful about contamination – soap down any surface that comes into contact with the raw chicken) and onion skins. Cover the bones with about 5 litres (170 fl oz) of cold water.

Bring to the boil, then reduce to a gentle simmer. Cook for at least 3 hours (between 3 and 5 hours is ideal). Refrain from stirring the soup during that time: the less you stir, the clearer the final broth will be. Skim off any foam that forms on the surface. After a couple of hours, season to taste with salt.

When the broth is golden, full of flavour and not watery, strain it and discard the solids. Cool and refrigerate; the stock will keep in the fridge for 3–4 days or you can freeze it to use at another time. Once it cools there will be a layer of hard yellow fat on the top of the soup. Lift the fat cap off before using the stock (you can save the fat to rub over chicken, to cook potatoes in or to add to ragus for extra flavour).

Pickled radishes and turnips

It's always good to have a jar of pickles or marinated things in the fridge. This is a simple pickle; it's not proper pickling, rather something my safta does to different vegetables she has in her fridge that are going soft or are a bit bruised. By covering radishes, cucumbers, cauliflower – almost any vegetable – in this pickling liquid she extends their lives. I like to spoon a large amount of labneh on a plate and spread it out so that it looks like a cloud, then top the plate with pickled radishes and turnips, some grilled spring onions and a few spicy pickled chillies that you can buy from Middle Eastern delis or Mediterranean grocery stores.

MAKES 1 JAR OF PICKLES

1 bunch of <u>radishes</u>, trimmed and sliced into quarters

1 bunch of <u>Hakurei turnips</u> or regular <u>round turnips</u>, trimmed and sliced into small pieces about 3 cm (1¼ in) wide

PICKLING LIQUID

2 teaspoons <u>salt</u>

500 ml (17 fl oz/2 cups) <u>water</u>

pinch of <u>sugar</u>

1 teaspoon <u>peppercorns</u>

3 <u>bay leaves</u>

1 teaspoon <u>fennel seeds</u>

60 ml (2 fl oz/¼ cup) plus 1 tablespoon <u>apple-cider vinegar</u>

Put all the ingredients for the pickling liquid except for the vinegar in a saucepan, stir and bring to a gentle boil. Reduce the heat to low and simmer for 5 minutes. Turn off the heat and leave the liquid to cool for about 20 minutes, then pour in the vinegar and stir. Put the radishes and turnips in separate containers, pour the liquid over them and leave to gently pickle at room temperature or in the fridge for at least 4 hours before serving.

Index

A

allium sauce 114

anchovies
   anchovy butter 96
   anchovy emulsion 134
   Crostini with stracciatella
     and two types of
     anchovy 51
   Pan-fried chicken thighs
     with green olives and
     pearl couscous 94
   Roast chicken with
     thyme, anchovy
     butter and
     potatoes 96–7
   sauce 94
   Spaghetti with whipped
     anchovy butter, garlic
     and chilli 170
   Sugarloaf cabbage with
     stracciatella and anchovy
     emulsion 134
   Whipped anchovy
     butter 67
anchovy butter 96
anchovy emulsion 134
apricots: Moroccan Rosh
   Hashanah lamb with
   prunes, apricots and
   honey 116–17
artichokes
   Boiled artichokes with
     vinaigrette 152
   how to eat 150
   Roman-Jewish–style fried
     artichokes 156–7
   Stuffed artichoke bottoms
     with onion and pea
     sauce 155
asparagus: Spring vegetables
   and toasted buckwheat
   with vinaigrette 146–7

B

beans
   beans 141
   Marinated borlotti
     beans 30
   Pappardelle with broad
     beans, peas and veal
     ragu 186–7
   Parmesan broth with
     borlotti beans and
     salsa verde 140–1
   String beans with
     lemon and dijon
     dressing 135
beef
   Minute steak with
     allium sauce 114–15
   see also veal
bell peppers *see* capsicums
berries *see* raspberries
biscuits
   Pistachio and
     almond amaretti
     biscuits 210
   Raiff 205
   Rugelach 206–9
Blistered, marinated
   capsicums 17
Boiled artichokes with
   vinaigrette 152
Braided challah 70–3
Braised beluga lentils with
   marinated silverbeet 144
braised lentils 144
bread
   Braided challah 70–3
   Focaccia 60–1
   Sesame focaccia
     flatbread 68–9
broths
   Parmesan broth with
     borlotti beans and
     salsa verde 140
   vegetable broth and
     chickpeas 118
   see also stocks
buckwheat: Spring
   vegetables and toasted
   buckwheat with
   vinaigrette 146–7
butters
   anchovy butter 96
   Whipped anchovy
     butter 67

Whipped confit garlic and
   tarragon butter 66
Whipped sesame seed and
   schmaltz butter 67
buying vegetables 130

C

cabbage: Sugarloaf cabbage
   with stracciatella and
   anchovy emulsion 134
capsicums
   Blistered, marinated
     capsicums 17
carrots
   Braised beluga lentils with
     marinated silverbeet 144
   braised lentils 144
   Chicken soup with
     matzah balls 100–5
   Chicken stock 228
   Marinated carrot salad 15
   My aunty's couscous with
     vegetables, chickpeas and
     vegetable broth 118–20
   vegetable broth and
     chickpeas 118
   Vegetable stock 227
   vegetables 118–20
Cavatelli with squid and
   XO sauce 185
cavolo nero *see* kale
celery
   Braised beluga lentils
     with marinated
     silverbeet 144
   braised lentils 144
   broth 140
   Chicken soup with
     matzah balls 100–5
   Chicken stock 228
   Fennel braised in parmesan
     broth 143
   My aunty's couscous with
     vegetables, chickpeas and
     vegetable broth 118–20
   Parmesan broth with
     borlotti beans and
     salsa verde 140–1

vegetable broth and
   chickpeas 118
Vegetable stock 227
chard *see* silverbeet
charred banana pepper and
   green chilli salsa 92–3
Charred eggplant with
   tahini and green chilli 23
cheese
   broth 140
   Conchiglioni with braised
     leek and cavolo nero
     green sauce 180–1
   Crostini with stracciatella
     and two types of
     anchovy 51
   Fennel braised in
     parmesan broth 143
   Grilled peaches with
     mozzarella and
     jamón 33
   Home-made labneh 224
   mascarpone 213
   Paccheri with tuna
     and guanciale
     amatriciana 188–9
   Pappardelle with
     broad beans, peas
     and veal ragu 186–7
   Parmesan broth with
     borlotti beans and
     salsa verde 140–1
   parmesan rinds 136
   Spaghetti with confit
     cherry tomato and
     fennel seeds 174–5
   Sugarloaf cabbage with
     stracciatella and anchovy
     emulsion 134
   Summer tomato, onion and
     pecorino crostata 122–3
   Vermouth poached cherries
     and mascarpone 213
cherries
   poached cherries 213
   Vermouth poached cherries
     and mascarpone 213
   Watermelon and cherries
     on ice 202

chicken
    Chicken livers and schmaltz onions on toast 42–3
    Chicken soup with matzah balls 100–5
    Chicken stock 228
    Matzah balls 105
    Pan-fried chicken thighs with green olives and pearl couscous 94
    Roast chicken with thyme, anchovy butter and potatoes 96–7
    schmaltz and crispy chicken skin 42
    schmaltz onions 42
    Whipped sesame seed and schmaltz butter 67
Chicken livers and schmaltz onions on toast 42–3
Chicken soup 102
Chicken soup with matzah balls 100–5
Chicken stock 228
chickpeas
    My aunty's couscous with vegetables, chickpeas and vegetable broth 118–20
    vegetable broth and chickpeas 118
chillies
    beans 141
    charred banana pepper and green chilli salsa 92–3
    Chraime with charred banana pepper and green chilli salsa 90–3
    confit tuna 48
    Garlic and chilli oil 223
    green chilli salsa 23
    matbukha 11
    Matbukha with prawn oil and grilled prawns 10–11
    Pan-fried chicken thighs with green olives and pearl couscous 94
    sauce 193
    Spaghetti with clams in garlic and chilli 176–7
    Spaghetti with confit cherry tomato and fennel seeds 174–5
    Tagliatelle with prawns and nduja pangrattato 192–4
    Vegetable stock 227
    zhoug 111

chocolate: Rugelach 206–9
Chraime with charred banana pepper and green chilli salsa 90–3
clams
    Spaghetti with clams in garlic and chilli 176–7
    Tins of preserved seafood, pickled vegetables, bread and good butter 51
colatura di alici 115
Conchiglioni with braised leek and cavolo nero green sauce 180–1
confit garlic and oil 66
confit tuna 48
Confit tuna, tomato and white onion salad 48–9
couscous
    couscous 118–20
    My aunty's couscous with vegetables, chickpeas and vegetable broth 118–20
    Pan-fried chicken thighs with green olives and pearl couscous 94
Crisp vegetables with lemon vinaigrette 29
crostata, Summer tomato, onion and pecorino 122–3
Crostini with stracciatella and two types of anchovy 51
cucumbers
    Crisp vegetables with lemon vinaigrette 29
    Dressed soft lettuce salad 149
cumin oil 111
Cured fresh sardines 47

D
dips
    tahini dip 23
dressings 48–9, 135, 149
    lemon vinaigrette 29
    mignonette 80
    nduja and tomato dressing 24
    see also vinaigrette 146, 152
Dressed soft lettuce salad 149

E
eggplants
    Charred eggplant with tahini and green chilli 23
    Preserved eggplant 14
eggs
    Fresh egg pasta 166–7
    Matzah balls 105
    mayonnaise 80–1
emulsion, anchovy 134

F
fennel
    Braised beluga lentils with marinated silverbeet 144
    braised lentils 144
    Fennel braised in parmesan broth 143
    prawn head stock 192
    Tagliatelle with prawns and nduja pangrattato 192–4
    Vegetable stock 227
fish
    Chraime with charred banana pepper and green chilli salsa 90–3
    Cured fresh sardines 47
    Fish cakes with green herbs and labneh 84
    Fried whitebait 46
    Kingfish crudo with a nduja and tomato dressing 24
    Seafood on ice with mayonnaise and mignonette 80–1
    Tins of preserved seafood, pickled vegetables, bread and good butter 51
    Whipped bottarga butter with fish roe 67
    Whole sea bream with thyme, capers and butter 86–7
    see also anchovies, tuna
Focaccia 60–1
Fresh cavatelli pasta 169
Fresh egg pasta 166–7
Fresh mint tea 202
Fried whitebait 46

G
garlic
    confit garlic and oil 66
    Garlic and chilli oil 223
    Whipped confit garlic and tarragon butter 66

glaze, honey and bay leaf 72–3
green chilli salsa 23
Grilled peaches with mozzarella and jamón 33

H
Home-made labneh 224
honey and bay leaf glaze 72–3

K
kale: Conchiglioni with braised leek and cavolo nero green sauce 180–1
kebabs, Minced lamb kebabs with zhoug, cumin oil and pickled red onion 110–11
Kingfish crudo with a nduja and tomato dressing 24

L
labneh, Home-made 224
lamb
    Lamb cutlets with pan sauce 106–7
    Minced lamb kebabs with zhoug, cumin oil and pickled red onion 110–11
    Moroccan Rosh Hashanah lamb with prunes, apricots and honey 116–17
    Stuffed artichoke bottoms with onion and pea sauce 155
leeks
    broth 140
    Conchiglioni with braised leek and cavolo nero green sauce 180–1
    Fennel braised in parmesan broth 143
    My aunty's couscous with vegetables, chickpeas and vegetable broth 118–20
    Parmesan broth with borlotti beans and salsa verde 140–1
    Spring vegetables and toasted buckwheat with vinaigrette 146–7
    vegetable broth and chickpeas 118
    Vegetable stock 227

lemon vinaigrette 29
lemon rind purée 135
lemons
  allium sauce 114
  Boiled artichokes with
    vinaigrette 152
  charred banana pepper and
    green chilli salsa 92–3
  dressing 135
  Fennel braised in
    parmesan broth 143
  Fish cakes with green
    herbs and labneh 84
  green chilli salsa 23
  lemon vinaigrette 29
  lemon rind purée 135
  Linguine with capers,
    bottarga and lemon 173
  mayonnaise 80–1
  nduja pangrattato 223
  Roman-Jewish–style fried
    artichokes 156–7
  sauce 94
  String beans with
    lemon and dijon
    dressing 135
  Stuffed artichoke bottoms
    with onion and pea
    sauce 155
  tahini dip 23
lentils
  Braised beluga lentils
    with marinated
    silverbeet 144
  braised lentils 144
  Linguine with capers,
    bottarga and lemon 173

M

marinade 106
Marinated borlotti beans 30
Marinated carrot salad 15
marinated silverbeet 144
mascarpone 213
matbukha 11
Matbukha with prawn oil
  and grilled prawns 10–11
Matzah balls 105
mayonnaise 80–1
melons see watermelons
mignonette 80
Minced lamb kebabs
  with zhoug, cumin
  oil and pickled
  red onion 110–11
Minute steak with allium
  sauce 114–15

Moroccan Rosh Hashanah
  lamb with prunes, apricots
  and honey 116–17
mushrooms
  broth 140
  Fennel braised in
    parmesan broth 143
  Parmesan broth with
    borlotti beans and
    salsa verde 140–1
  Vegetable stock 227
mussels: Tins of preserved
  seafood, pickled vegetables,
  bread and good butter 51
My aunty's couscous with
  vegetables, chickpeas and
  vegetable broth 118–20

N

nduja
  Kingfish crudo with a
    nduja and tomato
    dressing 24
  nduja and tomato
    dressing 24
  nduja pangrattato 223
  sauce 193
  Tagliatelle with
    prawns and nduja
    pangrattato 192–4
nuts
  Pistachio and almond
    amaretti biscuits 210
  Rugelach 206–9

O

oils
  confit garlic and oil 66
  cumin oil 111
  Garlic and chilli oil 223
  prawn oil 10
  tarragon oil 66
olives
  Pan-fried chicken thighs
    with green olives and
    pearl couscous 94
  Tins of preserved seafood,
    pickled vegetables, bread
    and good butter 51
onions
  onion and pea sauce 155
  pickled red onion 111
  schmaltz onions 42
oysters: Seafood on ice
  with mayonnaise and
  mignonette 80–1

P

Paccheri with tuna
  and guanciale
  amatriciana 188–9
pan sauce 106–7
Pan-fried chicken thighs
  with green olives and
  pearl couscous 94
Pangrattato 223
pangrattato, nduja 223
pantry 218–221
Pappardelle with broad beans,
  peas and veal ragu 186–7
Parmesan broth with
  borlotti beans and
  salsa verde 140–1
parmesan rinds 136
pasta
  Cavatelli with squid and
    XO sauce 185
  Conchiglioni with braised
    leek and cavolo nero
    green sauce 180–1
  cooking 163
  Fresh cavatelli pasta 169
  Fresh egg pasta 166–7
  Linguine with capers,
    bottarga and lemon 173
  Paccheri with tuna
    and guanciale
    amatriciana 188–9
  Pappardelle with
    broad beans, peas
    and veal ragu 186–7
  Spaghetti with clams in
    garlic and chilli 176–7
  Spaghetti with confit
    cherry tomato and
    fennel seeds 174–5
  Spaghetti with whipped
    anchovy butter, garlic
    and chilli 170
  Tagliatelle with
    prawns and nduja
    pangrattato 192–4
peaches: Grilled peaches
  with mozzarella and
  jamón 33
peas
  Dressed soft lettuce
    salad 149
  onion and pea sauce 155
  Pappardelle with
    broad beans, peas
    and veal ragu 186–7
  Stuffed artichoke
    bottoms with onion
    and pea sauce 155

Pickled radishes and
  turnips 229
pickled red onion 111
pickling liquid 229
Pistachio and almond
  amaretti biscuits 210
poached cherries 213
pork
  Grilled peaches
    with mozzarella
    and jamón 33
  Paccheri with tuna
    and guanciale
    amatriciana 188–9
  see also nduja
potatoes
  desiree potatoes 96
  Roast chicken with thyme,
    anchovy butter and
    potatoes 96–7
prawns
  Matbukha with prawn
    oil and grilled
    prawns 10–11
  prawn head stock 192
  prawn oil 10
  sauce 193
  Seafood on ice with
    mayonnaise and
    mignonette 80–1
  Tagliatelle with
    prawns and nduja
    pangrattato 192–4
Preserved eggplant 14
prunes: Moroccan Rosh
  Hashanah lamb with
  prunes, apricots and
  honey 116–17
pumpkin
  My aunty's couscous
    with vegetables,
    chickpeas and vegetable
    broth 118–20
purée, lemon rind 135

R

radishes
  Crisp vegetables with
    lemon vinaigrette 29
  Kingfish crudo with
    a nduja and tomato
    dressing 24
  Pickled radishes and
    turnips 229
ragu, Pappardelle with
  broad beans, peas and
  veal 186–7

Raiff 205
raspberries: Rugelach 206–9
Roast chicken with thyme, anchovy butter and potatoes 96–7
Roman-Jewish–style fried artichokes 156–7
Roman-Jewish–style fried zucchini with mint 18–20
Rugelach 206–9

S
salads
 Dressed soft lettuce salad 149
 Marinated carrot salad 15
 matbukha 11
salsas
 charred banana pepper and green chilli salsa 92–3
 green chilli salsa 23
 salsa verde 141
sauces 94, 193
 allium sauce 114
 onion and pea sauce 155
 pan sauce 106–7
 zhoug 111
 see also salsas
sausages *see* nduja
scallops: Seafood on ice with mayonnaise and mignonette 80–1
schmaltz and crispy chicken skin 42
schmaltz onions 42
Seafood on ice with mayonnaise and mignonette 80–1
seasoning throughout the cooking process 126
Sesame focaccia flatbread 68–9
silverbeet
 Braised beluga lentils with marinated silverbeet 144
 marinated silverbeet 144
snacking 36–9
soups
 Chicken soup with matzah balls 100–5
 Parmesan broth with borlotti beans and salsa verde 140–1

Spaghetti with clams in garlic and chilli 176–7
Spaghetti with confit cherry tomato and fennel seeds 174–5
Spaghetti with whipped anchovy butter, garlic and chilli 170
Spring vegetables and toasted buckwheat with vinaigrette 146–7
squid: Cavatelli with squid and XO sauce 185
stocks
 Chicken stock 228
 prawn head stock 192
 Vegetable stock 227
 see also broths
String beans with lemon and dijon dressing 135
Stuffed artichoke bottoms with onion and pea sauce 155
Sugarloaf cabbage with stracciatella and anchovy emulsion 134
Summer tomato, onion and pecorino crostata 122–3
sweet potatoes
 My aunty's couscous with vegetables, chickpeas and vegetable broth 118–20
 vegetables 118–20
Swiss chard *see* silverbeet

T
Tagliatelle with prawns and nduja pangrattato 192–4
tahini dip 23
tarragon oil 66
tea, Fresh mint 202
Tins of preserved seafood, pickled vegetables, bread and good butter 51
tomatoes
 Braised beluga lentils with marinated silverbeet 144
 Cavatelli with squid and XO sauce 185
 Charred eggplant with tahini and green chilli 23

Chraime with charred banana pepper and green chilli salsa 90–3
Confit tuna, tomato and white onion salad 48–9
Kingfish crudo with a nduja and tomato dressing 24
marinated silverbeet 144
matbukha 11
Matbukha with prawn oil and grilled prawns 10–11
nduja and tomato dressing 24
Paccheri with tuna and guanciale amatriciana 188–9
Parmesan broth with borlotti beans and salsa verde 140–1
prawn head stock 192
Spaghetti with confit cherry tomato and fennel seeds 174–5
Summer tomato, onion and pecorino crostata 122–3
Tagliatelle with prawns and nduja pangrattato 192–4
tuna
 confit tuna 48
 Confit tuna, tomato and white onion salad 48–9
 dressing 48–9
 Paccheri with tuna and guanciale amatriciana 188–9
turnips: Pickled radishes and turnips 229

V
veal: Pappardelle with broad beans, peas and veal ragu 186–7
vegetable broth and chickpeas 118
vegetable, buying 130
Vegetable stock 227
vegetables 118–20
Vermouth poached cherries and mascarpone 213
vinaigrettes 146, 152
vinaigrette, lemon 29

W
Watermelon and cherries on ice 202
Whipped anchovy butter 67
Whipped bottarga butter with fish roe 67
whipped butters 64–7
Whipped confit garlic and tarragon butter 66
Whipped sesame seed and schmaltz butter 67
Whole sea bream with thyme, capers and butter 86–7

Z
zhoug 111
zucchini
 My aunty's couscous with vegetables, chickpeas and vegetable broth 118–20
 Roman-Jewish–style fried zucchini with mint 18–20
 vegetables 118–20

Acknowledgements

This book is dedicated to my parents, Karen and Asher Bouhadana, who never had much themselves, but who gave me everything.

It is also for Rapha, my harshest critic, but always from a place of love.

Thank you to my Jewish family all over the world who generously shared the recipes and traditions of our ancestors with me – Doda Marcel, Dod Moize, Doda Raba Melani and all who came before. Thank you with all of my heart to my safta Rachel.

To my sisters, Ruby and Tahni. A thank you isn't enough for the hours of sistering you did to get me to where I am.

Thank you to Stephanie Stamatis, this book came together because of your mentorship. I am in awe of the way you set a scene, your taste, your tastebuds and your wisdom. I will always be grateful for your generosity and patience, it cannot be quantified.

Thank you to Lucia Bell-Epstein, who followed me from Rome to Melbourne, with suitcases full of chocolate and equipment, to shoot this book on film. Working with you, but more importantly, eating, travelling and playing made shooting this book easier than it should have been. I love seeing food through your eyes.

Thank you to Nye De Marchi for learning what makes me look sexy. You deserve credit for any time I look good in this book.

To everyone who tested my recipes – Callum Mitchell, Chris Yuille, Nye De Marchi, Ruby Bouhadana, Sophie Zilberman, Pete Baxter, Karen Bouhadana, Tali Sawicz, Debbie Mandelbaum and more – I am sure the readers of this book will be thankful for the hours you spent winding your way through my instructions.

Thank you to those who advised, supported and cooked with me and for this book – particularly Chris Yuille, Rushani Epa and Ziga Testen.

Thank you to Alice Kiandra-Adams, for welcoming Lucia and I into your Latteria Studio in Rome with such warmth and generosity. Thank you for trusting us with your kitchen, for all your help behind the scenes and for introducing us to the market and its beautiful vendors.

To Jack Shaw and Pete Baxter, I love building Hope St with you. Thank you for your belief, inspiration and food adventures, and for being my partners in the kitchen. Thank you for having my back at the restaurant while I spent time writing this book.

Thank you to my publishing house Hardie Grant for the support to breathe life into this book. Particularly to Eugenie Baulch, Alice Hardie-Grant and Tahlia Anderson.

To those who have followed my journey from Doorstep Deliveries, Crostini Kiosks, Ripponlea pop-ups, to Hope St and to here, I am so grateful.

About the Author

Ellie Bouhadana is an acclaimed self-taught chef who honed her skills in restaurants and at events in Melbourne. She gained popularity during the city's two and a half years of lockdown with her fresh pasta and pillowy focaccia packages called Doorstep Deliveries. Ellie's success led her to host a series of summer pop-up events and eventually become the head chef at Hope St Radio, a wine bar and radio station named by *Time Out* magazine as the 'third coolest bar in the world'. Famed for her flavourful and heartfelt cooking along with her focaccia, whipped butters, expertly pickled Moroccan carrots and nostalgic matzah ball soup. Inspired by her mixed Moroccan and Eastern European Jewish heritage and her love of the Mediterranean, her menu reflects food of the home, family traditions, and love of a full belly. Notably, Hope St Radio received acclaim from the *The Age Good Food Guide* that awarded them an impressive 4/5 stars, and honoured them with a coveted Chef's Hat, solidifying its reputation as a culinary destination and celebrating the unique and vibrant experience Ellie has created for her guests.

Published in 2024 by Hardie Grant Books,
an imprint of Hardie Grant Publishing

Hardie Grant Books (Melbourne)
Wurundjeri Country
Building 1, 658 Church Street
Richmond, Victoria 3121

Hardie Grant Books (London)
5th & 6th Floors
52–54 Southwark Street
London SE1 1UN

hardiegrant.com/books

Hardie Grant acknowledges the Traditional Owners of
the country on which we work, the Wurundjeri people
of the Kulin nation and the Gadigal people of the Eora
nation, and recognises their continuing connection to
the land, waters and culture. We pay our respects to their
Elders past and present.

A catalogue record for this
book is available from the
National Library of Australia
NATIONAL
LIBRARY
OF AUSTRALIA

Ellie's Table: Food from memory and food from home
ISBN 978 1 74379 875 1

10 9 8 7 6 5 4 3 2 1

PUBLISHERS: Alice Hardie-Grant, Tahlia Anderson
COMMISSIONING EDITOR: Rushani Epa
EDITOR: Eugenie Baulch
DESIGN MANAGER: Kristin Thomas
DESIGNERS: Longwen Wei, Celia Mance, Hardie Grant
Design Studio
TYPESETTER: Hannah Schubert
PHOTOGRAPHER: Lucia Bell-Epstein
CREATIVE DIRECTION AND STYLING:
Stephanie Stamatis
HOME ECONOMIST: Chris Yuille
HEAD OF PRODUCTION: Todd Rechner
PRODUCTION CONTROLLER: Jessica Harvie

Colour reproduction by Splitting Image Colour Studio
Printed in China by Leo Paper Products LTD.

FSC
MIX
Paper
FSC® C020056

The paper this book is printed on is from
FSC®-certified forests and other sources.
FSC® promotes environmentally responsible,
socially beneficial and economically viable
management of the world's forests.